A CHURCH THAT FLIES

TIM WOODROOF

A CHURCH THAT FLIES

A New Call to Restoration in the Churches of Christ

LEAFWOOD
PUBLISHERS

A Church That Flies
A New Call for Restoration in Churches of Christ
published by Leafwood Publishers

ISBN 0-9700836-1-0
Printed in the United States of America

Cover design by Rick Gibson

For information:
Leafwood Publishers
1409 Hunter Ridge
Siloam Springs, AR 72761
1-877-634-6004 (toll free)

Visit our website: www.leafwoodpublishers.com

03 04 05 06 07 08 09   7 6 5 4 3 2

Dedication

Writing is not a matter of putting words to paper.
Writing is a matter of putting thoughts to words.
I dedicate this book to Ron Stump who, time and again,
has helped me craft both the thoughts and the words.
Much of what follows is his.

Table of Contents

[T]he stream of national consciousness moves faster now, and is broader, but it seems to run less deep. The old channels cannot contain it and in its search for new ones there seems to be growing havoc and destruction along its banks. . . . I would like not to cut any new channels of consciousness but simply dig deeper into old ones that have become silted in with the debris of thoughts grown stale and platitudes too often repeated. "What's new?" is an interesting and broadening eternal question, but one which, if pursued exclusively, results only in an endless parade of trivia and fashion, the silt of tomorrow. I would like, instead, to be concerned with the question "What is best?," a question which cuts deeply rather than broadly, a question whose answers tend to move the silt downstream.

Robert Pirsig

Acknowledgements

Though writing is a solitary endeavor, "having written" is always a group exercise. To use a (tired?) metaphor, authoring a book is much like birthing a baby—one person goes through the labor, but lots of others encourage and advise and facilitate. I count myself fortunate that my delivery room was staffed with so many gifted and perceptive people. It would be less than gracious of me not to mention some of those who had an important role in shaping this work.

First, this book was born with the tender help of two midwives: the Westside Church of Christ in Beaverton, Oregon, and the Otter Creek Church of Christ in Nashville, Tennessee. I subjected both of these congregations to the messy process of thought-birth, with all the attendant sweating and groaning and frustrated pushing. In particular, my elders at Otter Creek read an incomplete manuscript before asking me to move to Nashville, and have patiently read the revisions made since. (Though they may prefer anonymity, I'd like to mention them by name: Steve Adams, Jim Butler, Mike Duncan, Fred Ewing, Terry Frisby, Jerry Masterson, Bill Reeder, Ed Rucker, David Shaub, and Fletcher Srygley.) Thank you. Corky French and Brandon Scott Thomas (my partners in ministry at Otter Creek) have been unselfish in their support of my writing. They carried a bigger burden so that I could spend time with my computer.

I was blessed to have several very competent and busy "doctors" attend the birthing process. These people dropped whatever they were doing to poke and prod and appraise the manuscript version of this newborn creation. They diagnosed more than a few problems that, caught early, were cleaned up with a little corrective surgery. Ruth Qualls, Doug Saunders, Lee Ann Rice, Jerry Franklin, Ross Cochran, Ken Neller, and Lowell Myers read various stages of the manuscript and offered encouragement and comment. My thanks to Jim and Louine Woodroof (my parents, yes, but also wise and perceptive readers). Mike Cope has always been gracious to read what I send him and respond in helpful ways. Thanks for your encouragement, Mike. I am grateful for the partnership of Leonard Allen, my publisher and editor for this particular effort, whose concern for the Spirit's role in the modern church deepened my own thinking and writing.

Two readers loved me enough to say that—in certain particulars—my baby was downright ugly. LaGard Smith helped me think more clearly about the arguments put forth in this book and pointed out language that was more evocative than needed. Mark Love pushed me hard on the dangers of pragmatism and the importance of incarnation in shaping a church. Each made a real contribution to this work—though, in the end, they may still consider this an ugly baby.

Finally, if I played "wife" in this little production, my wife played "husband." Her support and patience were critical all through the gestation period of this book. She wiped my brow and fed me ice chips for months at a time. I could not have done this without her active partnership and I want to honor her for that.

As you can see, many hands were involved in bringing this book to life. Still, most forewords insist that any errors or omissions or misstatements belong to the author alone. That's never made much sense to me. So instead, let me just say that, if you find something wrong with my baby, one of the above people is probably to blame. I will be happy to furnish you with their phone numbers and e-mail addresses.

Preface

This is a book written to members of the Churches of Christ as we begin a new millenium, facing all the challenges that changing times and circumstances present to God's people. It is written to, and in the context of, a church that is trying to find itself.

Some people claim this search is prompted by a kind of institutional senility—that the Churches of Christ are nearing the end of their productive life and are now engaged in a prolonged but inevitable decline.

I am not one of that number. While I agree that we are asking some very basic questions and searching for a renewed sense of identity, I see this search as a healthy sign of institutional adolescence. What we are engaged in as a movement is not an ending but a beginning. If we can be unafraid to ask the necessary questions and honest in giving truthful answers, there is a mature and productive adulthood awaiting those who engage the new millennium as members of this community of faith.

You have a right to know something about an author who would raise the issues addressed in this book. My great-grandfather was named Tolbert Fanning Woodroof (after the famous restoration preacher). My paternal grandfather preached for some 70 years for Churches of Christ in middle Tennessee. My father has preached for the last 45 years in Churches of Christ throughout the South and spent five years establishing a congregation in Christchurch, New Zealand. My maternal grandparents were pillars of the Union Avenue Church of Christ in Memphis, Tennessee. I have two uncles who preach and six uncles who have served as elders of various Churches of Christ. My sister and brother-in-law are on the mission field. A brother has spent his career at Harding. My siblings and cousins attended Church of Christ universities, as did I.

I am a child of our movement. My roots run deep in the Churches of Christ. I was nursed by, raised in, and shaped around the ideals of the restoration church. I owe a debt to the people and congregations of our fellowship I cannot even fathom, much less express.

For the past 17 years, I have followed an almost genetic call to preach. That time has been spent at three congregations: the 56th and Vine Church of Christ in Lincoln, Nebraska; the Westside Church of Christ in Beaverton, Oregon (a suburb of Portland); and, presently, the Otter Creek Church of Christ in Nashville, Tennessee. My most significant influences in ministry have been my fellow ministers in these works: James Hinkle, Glen Gray, and Ron Stump (to whom this book is gratefully dedicated). It has been my privilege to work with godly and loving elderships. I have written for our brotherhood papers and spoken at our brotherhood lectureships. I hope to spend the rest of my life serving the family of God that has done so much to serve me.

I want you to know these things about me because they provide a necessary context for reading this book. The issues I address in these pages are not easy or comfortable. They concern matters that we hold dear. These are subjects we care about and thus are sensitive to.

So I warn you from the outset: in places this book is critical of what we have done with the restoration plea and how we are con- ducting ourselves as a church. I hope you will remember that I offer these criticisms as someone who knows and loves the Church of Christ. I speak up in order to build up, not to tear down. I offer these observations out of a genuine sense of hope, not despair.

But this book is not just criticism. It is also prescription. I propose some things we can do to inject fresh life and renewed vitality into our members and our churches. Those possibilities arise out of my confidence in the people of this movement. We love the Bible. We want to be Christ-like. We yearn to be the church that God is calling us to be. Our strengths rather than our weaknesses prompt the writing of this book.

Here at the dawn of a new millennium, we have some "family matters" to discuss. But we should not fear that discussion. For in it are the seeds to new growth and a fresh phase in our development as God's people.

Tim Woodroof
Nashville, Tennessee
Spring 2000

Section I/ Orientation

Getting into a book is a bit like starting a friendship. There is that awkward time at the beginning when you don't know each other... you're not sure what each other has to say... you don't even know whether you're willing to make the investment real friendship requires.

So what do you do? You send out feelers. You strike up a conversation and watch how it goes. You question and test and evaluate. You talk about big picture things before you dive into the nitty gritty of real life.

The three chapters that follow are the beginnings of what I hope will be a prolonged discussion between us. They don't get into the nitty gritty of the subject we'll be talking about, but they do paint some big picture issues. They are intended to let you question and test and evaluate. They are meant to help you decide whether you want to make the investment a book like this requires.

The first chapter sets a metaphor I will play with throughout the book. It introduces you to "ornithopterists" and uses their experience to throw light on the condition of Churches of Christ today.

The second chapter suggests that our attempts to restore New Testament forms are at a dead end. Should we, therefore, throw the restoration ideal out of the window (as many seem willing to do)? Or should we determine rather to focus on restoring New Testament functions…to focus on the essential business of kingdom work?

The third chapter speaks to the need for a Christ-shaped church. It links the character of Christ to the character of the church. It insists that our Lord, not the church of prior times, should be the gravitational center of the church today.

These opening chapters will help you decide whether a more prolonged discussion is merited. They don't touch on every relevant issue—that's what the rest of the book is for. And they may raise more questions than they answer—be patient. But you should know, by the time you get through them, whether you want to meet again for further dialogue. I hope you will.

The church must be forever building,
and always decaying,
and always being restored.

T. S. Eliot

1/ Ornithopterists and Their Spiritual Cousins

It did not take the human race long to grow dissatisfied with the limits of gravity. Among the earliest narratives of recorded history—accounts of ancient legends and myths and dreams—are stories of men looking enviously at birds and coveting their ability to fly. It is impossible for those of us raised with airline schedules and moon-shots to appreciate how powerfully the dream of flight captured the imagination of ancient people.

For thousands of years, inventors and dreamers have thought about ways to build a flying machine that could lift humans into the heavens with the birds. Most of these dreamers made the assumption that to "fly" meant to soar not just *with* the birds but *like* the birds, by flapping some sort of mechanical wings. Historians of flight call such thinkers *ornithopterists* ("wing-flappers") because of their obsession with achieving flight by copying the way that birds fly.

From ancient Greek mythology, there is the story of Icarus who made wings fashioned of wood and feathers, held together by wax. By flapping mightily, Icarus was able to rise into the atmosphere and navigate the skies. Unfortunately, he flew so high and close to the sun that the wax melted and his feathers fell off, plunging Icarus into the Mediterranean where he drowned. (You can almost hear generations of mothers repeating this story to their children and

warning, "If God had wanted us to fly, he would have given us wings.")

In the fifteenth-century, Leonardo Da Vinci—fascinated with birds and the possibility of flight—sketched out a number of flying machines. His designs often betray the same confusion of form and function. In Leonardo's mind, flight would become possible by giving man equipment similar to that of birds: large wings, attached to the arms or driven mechanically by pedals and chains, that could be flapped up and down to achieve lift. There is no evidence that Leonardo ever built and tried one of his designs. If he had, he might have ended up like Icarus.

More centuries passed, and still the notion that a man-made flying machine would have to look and act like a bird dominated the thinking of inventors. Had the ornithopterists been successful in achieving flight through slavish imitation of the bird's form that would have been the end of the story. But an embarrassing string of failures and the deaths of numerous "aeronauts" proved that a flying machine—if it was to function—would have to be designed around a different form.

It wasn't until the last hundred years that inventors were finally able to disconnect function from form, and question whether flight might be possible without mimicking the manner in which birds achieved it. The Wright brothers, among others, decided not to focus on birds but on the problem of flight itself. Rather than attempting to build a better "flapper," they built one of the first wind tunnels to study the effects of wind on wings. With the handful of aerodynamic principles that resulted, they designed a machine to take advantage of those principles—whether it came out looking like a bird or not.

The rest, as they say, is history. On December 17, 1902, Wilbur and Orville flew their "Kitty Hawk Special" four times, the longest flight lasting 58 seconds. Their "flying machine" wasn't covered in feathers. It didn't have bird-shaped wings. The wings did not flap up and down.

But it flew.

How Do You Make a Church Fly?

In many ways, the history of the Churches of Christ has paralleled the history of flight. For the past one hundred and fifty years, we have looked enviously at New Testament churches and coveted their ability to fly. We gazed longingly at their loving fellowship, life-changing ethic, Spirit-led worship, and evangelistic witness. We noted the fervor of their faith and the courage that led them to the arena and the stake. We watched as a band of twelve grew into a church of three thousand and, then, matured into a movement that turned the world upside down.

Looking up at the early church, we grew dissatisfied with the limits of our own religious experience and yearned to fly with those first Christians. We dreamed of building a contemporary church that recaptured the same dynamic and faithfulness exhibited by the first-century exemplar. However, like the ornithopterists of old, we assumed that "function" was inextricably bound to "form"... that to fly *with* the first-century church required us to fly *like* it. In our minds, a restoration of the first-century spirit and dynamic would only be possible when we gave the modern church the same "equipment" as its ancient counterpart.

Copying first-century structures, organization, patterns and rituals became for us the best and necessary means for restoring the vitality and performance of the primitive church. If only we could reinstate the forms, function would follow. And so the past 150 years have been spent analyzing the New Testament church for "marks"

and "patterns."[1] Several generations of our ecclessiological ances-
tors have given their best to reincarnating the primitive model.
They poured over the available evidence, both biblical and historical, searching for the minutest clues regarding the behavior of
the early church. They dissected and classified and described
every detail of early church anatomy. They debated verb tenses
and necessary inferences.

Had we been successful in building a functional modern
church through slavish imitation of first-century forms, that
would have been the end of the story and there would be no
need for the ideological tug-of-war that is presently pulling at
our fellowship. But, as a movement, we have experienced an
embarrassing string of failures—divisions, stagnation, a sense of
being increasingly marginalized in our culture, a loss of identity,
and the spiritual deaths of people we know and love. We can't
seem to get the contemporary church off the ground—no matter how hard we flap our first-century wings.

Increasingly, the assumption that "function will follow the
restoration of correct forms" is being called into question. Many of
us are growing frustrated with a modern church that may look like
the ancient church in the particulars but fails to function with anything like its power and life-changing dynamic. Some are beginning
to ask whether it might be possible to be the Church of Christ today
without the focus on forms that has become our hallmark.

There is the nagging sense that our focus on the details of early
church life has dulled us to "the weightier matters" that animated
the spiritual walk of our first-century counterparts. We fear we
have become a people who major in the minors and minor in what
is truly major. We question whether the many issues that have
consumed us and dominated our discussions have grown out of all
proportion and diverted a movement that, at its inception,
addressed higher ideals.

If we are honest, however, the pressing motivation for ques-
tioning the way we do church is rooted less in our sensitivity to the

spiritually central than in the growing acknowledgement that our movement is no longer able to capture the imagination of a new generation. The issues that served as points of identification and rallying flags for the church through much of the last century, fail to ignite the passions of those who must carry the church into the next millenium. Increasingly, we find ourselves in the difficult position of holding a debate we do not want in order to secure a future we fear is slipping from us. As has been true of many movements before us, desperation is driving us where theology should but does not.

This book represents a small attempt to construct a spiritual "wind tunnel"—to study how the God who built Abram's family and the nation of Israel and the church of Pentecost might be working to build a faithful church today. Central to this endeavor (and no doubt problematic for some readers) is a willingness to disconnect form from function, to assert that function is primary, and to suggest it is possible to build a contemporary church that pleases God even if it does not look exactly like the church of the first or the nineteenth-century.

We want a church that flies. All the guilded models that capture the most intricate details of churches past are of little use to us if they cannot get off the ground. What is required is a church for today that soars with the same power and faith as the church of our first fathers. We don't need to build a better "flapper"—more accurate, more true to scale, more meticulously detailed. Rather, we should be concerned to build a church that is sensitive to the same "aerodynamic principles" that lifted the church in the first-century world, whether we end up looking like that church or not.

The church that results will not be dressed in first-century culture and attitudes. It will not meet in catacombs or adopt the worship patterns of the synagogue. It will not insist on recreating every facet of ancient church life and practice.

But maybe, just maybe, it will fly.

*Begin with the end
in mind.*

― Stephen Covey

2/ On a Mission from God

Oliver Sachs, in the title piece from his wonderful book *The Man who Mistook his Wife for a Hat*, tells of one of his neurological patients, Dr. P. This older gentleman—an accomplished musician, cultured and educated—developed a tumor in the visual cortex, resulting in strange and not-so-subtle problems. Dr. P. could dress himself, eat and carry on a conversation—until interrupted or distracted. Once the flow of his activity was broken, however, Dr. P. would freeze, motionless, staring unblinking into space. Having lost the thread of what he was about, Dr. P. came to a complete stop, forgetting himself and his surroundings. Only through gentle reminders of what he was doing and why could Dr. P. be persuaded to resume his activity.[1]

Movements, like people, can forget themselves. Interrupted or distracted, they can lose the thread that holds their activities together and gives them coherence. One moment we are marching along with a sense of purpose and identity. The next we are sitting paralyzed on the ground, wondering how we got here and where we are going. Something breaks into the flow of our activity and we find, to our surprise, that we can no longer recall what it was we were attempting to do.

The Churches of Christ are in such a period today. Somewhere along the way we have forgotten what we were doing and why. We find ourselves confused over the most basic questions: Who are we? and, What is our purpose? We've lost the thread that gives meaning to our activities, and, having done so, many of us have lost the motivation to continue doing what we no longer understand. We find ourselves paralyzed, not because we are too tired to go on but because we despair of our activity resulting in something that God values.

The purposes we *can* articulate for the church—borrowed as they are from a prior generation and a radically different world— seem narrow and rote. In quiet and reflective moments, we question whether those goals are worthy of the sacrifices required. Many of us are no longer willing to pour the best of ourselves into the preservation of nineteenth-century modes of worship or doctrinal positions that, in our hearts, we no longer accept or believe to be central. Jesus did not die, nor do we want to live, to ensure that buildings not have kitchens or that music remain congregational and acappella or that a woman never make announcements in church.

The debate over such matters is exhausting precisely because it seems so irrelevant. The world around us is sick and demented. Daily, we watch people being butchered and starved and exploited. Children are growing up fatherless. The greed of nations is devouring entire populations in mindless wars. "Sexual ethics" is oxymoronic and increasingly anachronistic. Politicians are corrupt; priests are perverse; and "there is violence in the land." It will take something more potent than correct positions on worship etiquette to make a dint in this present darkness.

And we know it.

Yet, from some memory older than the restoration plea or even than Christianity itself, comes the notion that the people of God *should* make a difference, a difference felt at the foundations of our culture. Whatever our purpose and mission, we know that it should be no little thing concerned with the fringes of life. If something is to break into our paralysis and startle us once more into activity, we must find a mission that is worthy of renewed efforts.

How Do You Spell Restoration?

When I write of a "church that flies," it is precisely this sense of mission that is in mind. In order for Churches of Christ to soar into the third millennium with vigor, a recovery of purpose is required. Our fellowship, in short, needs to know that it is still on a mission from God.

An effective, functioning, faithful church... a church that makes a difference... a church whose priorities and purposes serve the kingdom of God... *that* church must understand who it is, where it is going, what it values, and why it exists.

For decades, the notion that we were a "restoration people," called to "do Bible things in Bible ways," provided that sense of mission. We prided ourselves on replicating in modern times the ancient and primitive rites of first-century faith and practice. We were consumed with the identification and cataloguing of the early churches' modes of worship, examples of outreach and cooperation, their structures for leadership, the names by which they called themselves, the ethical standards by which they lived, and the means by which they expressed and maintained community. We believed that by becoming students of the early church and by adopting those ancient patterns of life for ourselves, we could restore the ancient church in modern times.

The duplication of the manner in which the earliest Christians "did church" became for many of us *the* central tenet of restoration efforts. The result of all those years of study and discussion was a real (if informal) consensus about how the first-century church acted and how, therefore, we ought to act. Did they take the Supper every first day of the week? That pattern was seen as binding on any church that would be faithful today. Did they have five acts of worship? So must we, and neither less nor more. Did they have elders and deacons chosen on the pattern of 1 Timothy 3 and Titus 1? We must also have both elders and deacons (never one without the other), and those must be chosen strictly by the standards set out in the pastoral epistles. Did they have love feasts and greet each other with a holy kiss and speak in tongues during their worship services? Well, you can't take restoration too far!

But, of course, we did. Having gotten the restoration bit between our teeth, it was hard to know where to stop. How many cups did early Christians use for the Supper? Was the bread they used one loaf or bite-sized pieces? Where was the biblical authority for a Sunday School or cooperative support for children's homes or a Missionary Society? Did early churches build church buildings or hire located ministers? Was it proper to erect family life centers and hold marriage seminars and feed hungry people who wouldn't sit still for a Bible lesson?

It was precisely over such questions that Churches of Christ have, for the past hundred years, reasoned and debated and argued. Eventually it was over such questions that we alienated and divided. To the outside observer, all this frenzy about ancient patterns and modern practice seems obtuse and even absurd. What such an observer would fail to understand is the critical assumption we were making even as we split over these theological hairs.

The assumption, rooted in no less a figure than Alexander Campbell, was that if we could replicate the ancient church in modern times the millenium would be ushered in. For Campbell, restoration was no mere tool for getting the church back on track. It would open the door for the return of Christ and the judgment of the world.[2] If only the first-century church could be resurrected, if only all people of good character would join together in practicing simple, primitive Christianity stripped of the accumulated theological baggage of the centuries, the path would be cleared for the promises of God to be fulfilled *in toto*.

Function Follows Form?

Of course, that was *Campbell's* assumption, not ours. As good amillenialists, we could not swallow Campbell's theories about the end times. But we could (and did) modify his assumption to one with which we were more comfortable. Why was it so important to conform our practice of church to the patterns and forms of the first-century? *Because when we perfectly restored the first-century pattern, we believed we would usher in a revival of first-century power and effectiveness.* Function would follow form. We convinced ourselves that the power, harmony, fervor, and holiness we saw in the ancient church would break out afresh in the modern church—if only we could reinstate the pattern they followed. By "doing church" in the same way the ancients "did church," we too could become a church that turned the world upside down, changed lives and brought glory to God.

That was the assumption behind our perplexing obsession with the details of first-century church life. We did not study the past because we liked it better than the present. We scoured the past because we saw it as our best hope for functioning effectively in the here-and-now. Copy the modes of early worship and true worship would break out among us. Imitate the methods of early evangelism and the world (or at least the interested) would beat a path to our door. Model our leadership structure and styles after those found in Jerusalem or Antioch or Ephesus and God would bless us with leaders who were leaders indeed.

So captivated were we by this assumption regarding restoration that we took matters a step further. Not only would the pursuit of form lead us to function, but *only* the pursuit of form would do so. Only by discovering and reproducing the modes, methods and practices of the first-century church could we have any assurance that the resulting church would produce the fruit God wanted. There could be no legitimate leadership in the church, no trustable vision and divinely sanctioned authority, unless such leadership grew out of the New Testament pattern of elders, deacons, and evangelists.

There could be no legitimate worship, no true praise or pleasing sacrifice, unless that worship matched exactly in form and expression the patterns seen in the early church. There could be no legitimate evangelism unless, first and foremost, the means, methods, and message used by the modern evangelist conformed precisely to the express or necessarily implied example of his ancient counterpart.

Unless the form was correct, the results didn't count.

Thus we found an ingenious way to kill two birds with one Bible. What is our mission? We are the ones who have discovered the key to revival for the church. Because we worship like the first churches and organize ourselves like them and adhere strictly to their ethic and do not practice any unauthorized "innovations," God is using us to rebuild in these last days a church through which he can freely work.

And what about all those other churches out there? Well, sadly, the good that they do is tainted because they are not doing it in the right way. Certainly, there are churches that have a powerful ministry of compassion for the poor, but because they are encumbered with a denominational structure, God will not bless their efforts or use them to expand his kingdom. And, yes, there are groups that have stressed the deepening of the spiritual life through prayer and confession; but they are unsound on the instrumental music question, so their spiritual wisdom is suspect. And there are examples in the religious world around us of harmonious fellowship, holy living, sincere worship, sacrificial generosity, and dedicated service. All that wasted on the kingdom, however. Because they fall short on the *means*, the *ends* cannot be valid.

Inspecting Our Fruit

All of which might be quite defensible if we could point to the results of our own efforts and show that, in fact, *function has followed form for us*. If the Churches of Christ could demonstrate that our key does indeed fit the lock for effective churches, that after 150 years of pursuing proper form we were finally functioning as the loving, holy, evangelistically fervent, compassionate, worshipful body of Christ envisioned by the apostles, there might be room for boasting about ourselves and discounting the efforts of others.

So what has been our fruit? I take nothing away from the good done in our fellowship over the years: the souls that have been won, the lives that have been changed, the sacrifices that have been made, the worship that has been offered. Yet enough time has passed, enough effort has been invested to allow the question, "Are we now functioning as the glorious church we want so badly to be?"

Has our obsession with New Testament patterns and duly authorized forms resulted in a more loving and united community? Having struggled so long with issues of church leadership, do we now provide a vivid and compelling model of strong, faithful, visionary leadership for the religious world around us? After all the dust has settled from our arguments over modes of baptism and issues surrounding discipleship, are we turning the world upside down with our passion to save the lost?

Forced to admit that our movement has, in fact, stagnated, that we have divided ourselves into exhaustion, that we have not enjoyed the expected period of explosive growth, that our young people are leaving (or at least have discovered little passion for the vision which captured their fathers), that our worship periods have settled into a stultifying sameness, that our congregations are graying at a rapid rate or dying off entirely, a strange kind of rear-guard action is taking place in many quarters. Unwilling to accept that our assumptions about restoration may have been wrong, we are scrambling to find ways to shift the blame. It is not our efforts that have been misdirected, it is the times in which we live! We console ourselves with memories of Jeremiah's lonely ministry and Jesus' inability to perform miracles in Nazareth because of the people's "lack of faith." We tell ourselves that it is hard to be right, and quote like a mantra "narrow the road that leads to life, and *only a few* find it." Our present struggles have become almost a badge of honor, proving in a perverse way that we are on the right path—it's just that nobody is interested in the truth any more.

The prescription for the church advocated by those who take this tack is for the church to hunker down, protect its gains, remain "faithful" especially in these difficult days—and (God help us) do more, much more, of the same thing we have been doing. If only we hang on, God will eventually bring the blessing we have all been taught to expect.

The Loyal Opposition

Not everyone, however, is taking that line. Some of us, reviewing the state of Churches of Christ at the dawn of the twenty-first century, are recognizing that drastic surgery is in order or else the patient may well expire on the table. To *do* more of the same will *result* in more of the same, and *that* we cannot afford. It is time to do something different so that we can make a difference.

These voices calling for change will not let our movement take refuge by circling the wagons against a hostile world. They refuse to shift the blame to a hardhearted culture or an increasingly unfaithful church. They remind us that if first-century Christians had heard Jesus' words about the "narrow road" in the same way we seem to be hearing them, there would have been no evangelistic push out of Jerusalem, no turning the world upside down. They still have faith that the Churches of Christ can find a way to function effectively in these dark times. As a consequence, they are far more willing to call into question the assumptions our movement has made about restoration and to wonder whether there might be another way to "do church" today than focusing on and imitating New Testament forms.

For a new generation in our churches (and for many in the older generation, I quickly and gratefully acknowledge), a critical decision has been made: *function comes first, not form.* These people yearn to be a Christ-like, Spirit-led, sanctified, disciple-making community that makes a difference in the world. For them, the only kind of restoration worth pursuing has little to do with resuscitating ancient methods and much to do with recapturing an ancient vision of who God's people are and what business they are to be about. They no longer believe that a restoration of proper forms will ensure proper functioning in the church. That belief has been beaten out of them by too many years of experience with churches consumed with forms and oblivious to the essential functions of God's people. They are convinced, instead, that it is those "essential functions" that must consume our attention.

Ask them if they are interested in restoring the first-century church and they will answer, "Yes!" But ask them *what* about the first-century church they want to restore, and you will hear things like "their passionate worship," "their effective outreach," or "their sense of community." Restoration, for this generation, isn't about how the first-century church did business. It's about *what* business that church did. They would say that we should be focusing on core values, not tinkering with matters that are peripheral and tiny. "Form follows function," they will insist. "Get the functions right and God will provide the forms we need to do His business effectively."

And they want to be biblical. Only being "biblical" means paying attention to the "weightier matters of the law" rather than being tyrannized by the details. (See Chapter Eight.) They have seen too many people in the Bible and in the modern church who have focused on twigs and missed the forest. They realize that "correctness" is not the same as "godliness," that doing things right is not synonymous with doing the right things. Being biblical, for them, means pursuing the same ends as the apostles and the first-century church, not using the same methods or adopting the same forms.

In fact, they confront us with a most difficult question. "Who is being more biblical? Who is really being faithful? The church that adopts innovative and creative methods of building a strong sense of community among its members, or the church that is so wedded to particular forms it cannot effectively build loving relationships? The church that encourages a personal encounter with God through music, drama, testimonial, and dialogue, or the church that sticks to traditional worship formats whether or not they help members experience God? The church that is known in its neighborhood for feeding and housing battered women, or the church that is unknown by its neighbors because it cannot find biblical authority for using church funds for such activities?"

Those who are part of this ground swell in the Churches of Christ are as passionate about restoration as those who have gone before. We are as taken with the power and vitality of the first-century church as were our parents. We, like them, believe that churches in Jerusalem and Antioch and Ephesus and—yes—even Corinth are worthy of our intense study and faithful imitation.

The difference is that we want most to restore the *functions* to which God has called his people, and are willing to disconnect first-century forms from those timeless functions. We believe it is possible to experience again the power and life-changing dynamic of the early church, but only if we are able to find fresh wineskins to contain the gospel that is always new.

We want the chance to build a church that flies. In many ways, the church that results will not look like the ancient church. It will use forms and methods and approaches that would never have occurred to Christians in Philippi or Rome. It will draw from a contemporary toolbox rather than an exclusively ancient one. It will meet present needs using a mix of methods both ancient and modern.

What that church will have in common with the first churches is a commitment to being the people God wants us to be, doing the work God gives us to do, living the lives God calls us to live. Our methods may vary, but our goals are the same. Our means may differ, but our ends are identical. Our forms will be fresh, but the same functions hold for us as for them.

We long for the chance to build a church that flies *with* the ancient church. From the outset, we confess that the church we envision will not fly *like* its first-century counterpart in every respect. But in the end, we believe it is a functioning church that is important to God—whatever forms that church adopts.

That is a goal that has, I believe, the power to capture the children of the Restoration Movement. It is an ideal bold enough to break into our paralysis and startle us once more into activity. It promises to breathe new life into people who have lost their way and forgotten their purpose. By rediscovering the ancient purposes that have always shaped God's people in the past, and committing to the pursuit of those purposes in the present, we have hope of remembering what we are about and resuming our interrupted activity.

To set as our goal the reproduction of a given first-, tenth-, or eighteenth-century church as the means to being Christ's body would be as unwise upon reflection as someone's misguided belief that buying a house, furniture, and car like those of his happily married friend will provide him a good marriage. That man should put his energies into finding a woman to love rather than to building and decorating. Similarly, our goal of being the body of Christ must derive from a personal relationship with him rather than from a reproduction of form, ritual, and methodology.[1]

Rubel Shelly & Randall Harris

3/ The Christ-Shaped Church

Almost thirty years ago, I visited the Louvre in Paris. I wandered through the rooms and hallways, looking at the great works of art and admiring the incredible talent of some of history's greatest painters.

Strangely, my most vivid memory of that visit is not the Mona Lisa or the works of Picasso and Rembrandt hanging from the walls. I recall, rather, small knots of painters, huddled with their canvases and oils in front of those masterpieces, copying the works of painters long dead. They created incredibly faithful reproductions, duplicating exactly the colors, brush strokes, and perspectives of the originals. It was obvious that these people had great talent. They could have painted anything. But there they were, squinting in the shadows of another painter's creation, copying his copy of life.

When I asked a guide why they were there, he responded that some were students, honing their technique at the feet of the masters. But others made an entire career from painting and selling such reproductions. Evidently, there was a brisk market for skillfully rendered copies.

I watched them working and was overwhelmed by sadness. So much talent. So much skill. Yet some of those artists would never create an original work of art. They were enslaved to a precise mimicry of artists who had gone before them. No matter how careful and exacting their work, it would always be derivative, a copy. While the Masters looked at life—a beautiful woman, a lush landscape, an historical moment—and captured what they envisioned with paint, these lesser artists were content to copy canvases.

The Second Incarnation

The chapters that follow must be read through the lens of this single thought: the fundamental dynamic at work in the faithful church—shaping its character, forming its mission, setting its priorities—is the divine imperative that the church incarnate Christ.

First-century churches understood themselves as extensions of the life and ministry, the personality and priorities of their Lord. They were his body, his aroma in the world, his fullness, his ambassadors and representatives (Rom. 12:4ff; 1 Cor. 12:12ff; Eph. 1:22-23; Col. 2:19). "Christ in you" became not only a motivating force for personal behavior, but the sure pattern shaping these early communities of faith.

Shelly and Harris, then, are correct when they identify the church as the "second incarnation" of God on the earth.

Just as he was God incarnate in a physical body as Jesus of Nazareth, so is he now God incarnate in a spiritual body as the church. When that church is healthy and engaged in its proper work, it becomes Christ's very presence in the world. It carries on what he started among us. It is the grand finale to his ministry and is his chosen vehicle for living in the world in fullness rather than in mere memory.[2]

Our hands are God's hands; our mouths are God's mouth. We are all being transformed into his image and—collectively—radiate his glory for the world to see. God has taken up residence in his church and manifests his glory through us. The church is Jesus wrapped in the fleshly covering of our own feeble selves.[3]

Many Christians—who would never for a moment doubt that Jesus is God in the flesh—have no understanding that the church is also called to enflesh God. Yet such an understanding is vital if we are to discover our true nature and discern our true work. Who are we? We are a people shaped in the "image" of our master; we embody Christ's character and essence; we personify Jesus. What is our work? To carry on the ministry and mission of our Lord; to portray in our world his passions and priorities.

I can think of no more practical guide for modern disciples as they attempt to shape the present church along ancient lines. If the church is intended to incarnate Jesus, then surely Jesus himself provides the basic pattern that shapes the church.

Again, Shelly and Harris:

> Is the activity or methodology under contemplation consistent with the person and work of Jesus Christ? If we do this, will the people who see it think we reveal Christ? Will we be doing what people would expect to see Christ doing in this situation?
>
> This principle has broad consequences for ecclesiology. It says, for example, that the church need not have either explicit mandate or permission for everything it wishes to do. The church may confidently ground its activities…in the character of her head.[4]

Jesus exercises his influence over the church today not primarily by ancient precedent but through his Spirit and by the magnetic attraction of his personality and priorities. As we know him better, we are drawn to look more like him. As we imitate what we see in him, we become his presence in ever more tangible ways.

As an example, imagine a church that was willing to shape itself by Jesus' understanding of his own mission. He makes a number of "I have come" statements that reveal his own priorities, his own sense of kingdom business. "I have come to call sinners...to serve and to give my life...to preach good news...to do the will of my Father...to bring judgment...so that the blind will see and those who see will become blind...so that they may have life...as a light...to save the world... to testify to the truth."[5]

The Christ-shaped church would be drawn to making those priorities its own. At the center of its life together would be a concern for the lost, for preaching good news, for selfless service and obedience to God, for being light in a dark world. By looking at what was important to Jesus (his need for prayer and worship, his concern to train disciples, his instinct for the spiritually central and impatience with matters that were peripheral or distracting), it is possible to shape a church that honors the same things Jesus did.

This direct linkage to the character of Christ allows the faithful church to root itself firmly in its Lord. Ecclessiology arises principally from the pages of the Gospels in such a church, rather than from Acts or the Epistles. It can be argued there is not as much guidance about *how* to worship or serve or witness (what specific means and methods to use) in the books of Jesus as there is in the books of the church. But perhaps *how* the early church attempted to incarnate Jesus in their time and culture is not as important a lesson for us as learning *what* it is about Jesus they (and we) should incarnate.

When it is all too easy for us to shape the church in our own image, this incarnational principle would remind us that the church is intended to manifest *Christ*—to reflect *his* character, not ours. While we are tempted to allow the priorities of our culture or our religious milieu or even the restoration ideal to set an agenda for the church, this principle would force us to recognize that Christ lived out his own set of priorities, which take precedence over all others, no matter how well-intentioned. And though we might want to identify ourselves by distinctive doctrines or distinguishing religious practices, a church focused on incarnating Christ will acknowledge that what most identifies any people of God as the people of God is a consuming passion to pursue those things that are closest to the heart of God's son.

We are the Church *of Christ*, and it is *his* nature that, in the end, must shape our own. Whatever forms the church uses in its assemblies, whatever programs it adopts for ministry, whatever means it uses to express fellowship, the result must be something so Christlike, so reflective of his character, so *incarnational* that we remind ourselves and our world of the man we meet in the Gospels. This call to embody our Lord in the church serves as a theological umbrella, an overarching imperative for the people of God no matter what aspect of church is under discussion. Failing at this point is to fail at the one point where failure is fatal.

The Church and the Forces of Gravity

Somewhere along the line, the restoration ideal has been used to convince Churches of Christ that the life of the modern church should revolve around the life of the ancient one. What is our task? To replicate in these last days the church we find in the first century; to be now what they were then; to imitate the early church and shape ourselves after the pattern we find there.

The result? The church of the first-century has become our gravitational center. We revolve around the ancient church and allow it to set the agenda for our churches today. When it comes to our understanding of the church, we have expended far more time and effort exploring "patterns" in New Testament congregations than searching out priorities in the life of our Lord.

If Churches of Christ are to survive with any kind of vigor and effectiveness in the twenty-first century, we must consciously choose to stop being a moon revolving around the planet of the ancient church. All along, the ancient church itself was doing what we should be doing—revolving around the bright and shining center of the spiritual solar system, the Son of God. It is not unfaithfulness to break away from the satellite to be caught up in Jesus himself. It is not unfaithfulness to establish our own orbit around him.

Jesus Christ, not the early church, is the gravitational center of the church. Our task is to incarnate *him*, not *it*. Our task is to become *him*, not *them*. It is his personality, his mission, his ministry, his priorities, his relationships, his cross and resurrection that are the leading, shaping, directional forces at work upon us as a church. We exist to look like him. We exist to live like him. We exist to be his presence in this world.

Jesus Christ is the church's black hole. We are caught in his gravitational pull. We revolve around him, spiraling ever closer to him, until (at last) we become one with him—indivisible, indistinguishable, Christ is all and is in all (Col. 3:11).

This is not mere semantics. It addresses the most critical need, the most pressing hunger, among those of us who are members of the Churches of Christ today. For it has become increasingly clear that, while the ancient church might provide a pattern for us, it cannot supply power. It can suggest methodology, but it cannot produce transformation.

Yet it is power we need—both in our churches and in our individual lives. It is transformed living (in community and in our personal walks) for which we are hungry.

To set as our goal the restoration of ancient church practices and polity puts the focus squarely on what *we* do: how well *we* understand the pattern; how correctly *we* implement it in our churches; how carefully *we* guard against unauthorized innovations. And, in the end, such a focus limits available power to that which we generate ourselves. Our diligence becomes the engine that drives the modern church.

But to set as our goal the incarnation of Christ in our lives and churches puts the focus squarely on what God is doing in us. Such a goal takes seriously the role of the Holy Spirit as the source of and power for transformation among the people of God. It reminds us that God's grace has never depended on our correctness to make us right. It teaches us that incarnation is a mystery to which we submit, not a program for us to implement. It thrills us with the good news that there is a bubbling power available to us that transcends our earnest diligence.

When Jesus Christ is allowed to be the gravitational center of his church, when his Spirit is recognized and welcomed, when grace is permitted to do its motivating work in our lives, an inexhaustible source of energy and power becomes available for us.

For that, if for no other reason, a change of focus is required, and a change of orbit is demanded.

Why this Matters for Reading this Book

This is a book about rediscovering purpose as a church. It addresses matters like what our business is as the people of God and what means we can use to accomplish kingdom ends. Lots will be said about religious "forms" and essential "functions."

But the necessary context for understanding this book is the idea that the church is supposed to incarnate Christ. It's why I call into question our reliance on "pattern theology" (rather than a thoughtful Christology) for shaping the church. It's why I resist the notion that the early church (rather than Christ himself) should be our defining focus.

It's why I write about the *functions* of Christ's church. Jesus could speak with confidence about *why* he had come and *what* he had been commissioned to do. We should have that same confidence about our essential business. As you will see, I believe that business clusters around the functions of worship, holy living, building community, training disciples, serving, witnessing, and influencing our world. These functions were not chosen arbitrarily. They are rooted in an understanding of what Jesus saw his own mission to be. Certainly, we see these same functions reflected in the life and ministry of the early church. But our confidence that these functions comprise the essential business of the modern church derives from our *Lord's* life and ministry rather than any "pattern" of early church behavior.

And this is why, ultimately, I distinguish between those functions and the forms we use to express them. You may read these pages and imagine that I am disdainful of religious forms, that I would abandon them all. That is not my intent. It is impossible to practice faith without forms. We will always require routine and ritual—shared habits and practices—to enact our common commitment to God. It is not forms *per se* I reject, but forms that have lost connection with their Head—thoughtless, reflexive, ineffectual, outmoded forms that fail to communicate Christ and mediate grace, forms that say more about Corinth and Jerusalem (or nineteenth-century America) than about Jesus. We are to define ourselves by the character and mind of Christ, not by a finite set of religious forms, enacted in particular ways and at particular times.

You may also understand me to say that old forms should be abandoned and new ones adopted. Again, that is not my intent. Some ancient forms (notably baptism and the Supper) are so enmeshed with the core gospel as to be irreplaceable. To let go of the form would subject us to significant theological loss. At the same time, some new forms (e.g., a few of the contemporary songs we sing, "consumer driven" models of church growth, the move toward sound bites rather than sermons) are shallow and unworthy of the cause for which they are enlisted. There are ancient forms that merit constant picking up and dusting off and re-valuing. And there are some contemporary forms that should be consigned to the dust-bin as rapidly as possible. New is not always better. But simply because religious forms have the patina of antiquity does not ensure that holding onto them will make us a "faithful" people. Forms are intended to help us function faithfully. When old forms cease to be effective and relevant and life-changing, faithfulness may well demand that we abandon them in favor of more contemporary methods for getting at the church's essential business.

Finally, you will find yourself struggling (as I do) with the healthy dose of "pragmatism" that permeates the pages to follow. I will speak repeatedly about "effectiveness" and whether what we do "works." I believe that the religious forms we use must promote true worship and holiness, must foster intimate community and mature disciples, must encourage meaningful service and powerful witness and significant influence in our world. I challenge the assumption that, if we have the "correct" forms, effective function will result. We must begin with the question, "What business does God call us to?" and then ask, "How can we effectively accomplish that business?" But the "effectiveness" I want to explore has little to do with tickling modern ears and sensibilities. It cannot be measured by numbers. It is an effectiveness measured incarnationally. As Americans living at the dawn of the third millennium, how can we best promote Christ-likeness? How can we, in contemporary times, build a Christ-shaped church?

My skills as a writer are not sufficient to prevent misunderstandings and avoid wrong impressions. Because the issues addressed are issues we care about deeply, the potential for misstatement and overstatement is great. You will not agree with some (perhaps much) of what you read. But, at the heart of this book is something we are all concerned about—"How can we be a church that honors Christ, that is shaped by his character and priorities, and that accomplishes the kingdom business he came to do?" You may answer the question differently than I. But the question itself is worthy of being asked. It is the question that we as a movement must ask at this particular juncture of our history. I am not sure we are asking that question seriously enough. I am quite sure we have not answered it satisfactorily.

Rendering Jesus

As we paint on the canvas of the modern church, we have a choice to make. What will we focus on? What model will we use to craft our understanding of how the church today should look?

We can arrange our canvas and oils in front of the portraits of the church painted in Acts and Philippians and the Corinthian correspondence. We can expend our time, energy, and talents duplicating exactly the colors, strokes, and perspectives of those first-century churches. We can imitate their imitation of Jesus.

Or we can take our canvas to the Gospels and set it in front of the Original himself. Our palette will draw from his personality. Our lines and shapes will attempt to capture his characteristics. Certainly, we will draw from the wisdom and example (and learn from the mistakes) of those who have gone before, who have preceded us in the attempt to paint a Christ-shaped church.

But, in the end, the church we paint will be based on our understanding of Jesus, not just their understanding of him. Our attempt will be to faithfully render his likeness in our churches, not their likeness. And when people look over our shoulder to see what we are creating, what they will see is our attempt to faithfully portray our Lord, rather than a meticulous reproduction of the ancient church's portrayal of him.

By definition, that is a creative and risky endeavor. It requires us to color outside the lines of our heritage. It demands shadings and perspectives that are unique to ourselves and our times. It makes it possible for carelessness or thoughtlessness or sinfulness to mar our portrait and distort our depiction of the Master.

But if you believe that the Spirit has his hand on the brush we hold, if you accept that the God of grace is painting with us, if you trust that the one who stands before us as model is also within us—informing and empowering our portrait—we can be bold. Of such stuff, masterpieces are made.

Section II / Form, Function, and the Churches of Christ

The Churches of Christ are attempting to fly in turbulent times today. Suspended in the opening years of twenty-first-century America, we find ourselves buffeted by crosswinds we have never experienced before. Those cross currents force us to rethink styles of preaching and teaching, the issues we must address, the kinds of ministry in which we engage, the nature of our relationships, and even the lenses through which we read Scripture. There are calls to update worship styles to permit contemporary worshippers to express themselves more sincerely. There is a growing recognition that we are not having the impact on the world around us that we should—and a growing consensus that we must adapt our methods to changed circumstances. We are reassessing everything from leadership styles to community involvement to long-cherished doctrinal positions.

Increasingly, we are aware that present times differ significantly from the first-century world of the New Testament—or even the nineteenth-century world in which our movement was born. For some, that difference highlights a clear call for the church to hold the line and refuse to "compromise" with the world by making any changes whatever. Others believe that, unless changes are made, we will cease to speak to our world (and eventually ourselves) with the life-changing message that "Jesus saves."

All of us want to be true to the biblical winds that blow across the centuries. Should we, to be a faithful church, simply ignore the times in which we live so as to protect the shape of the church we have inherited from our fathers? Or must we recognize that, to be an effective community of faith in these turbulent days, we are required to make changes in form so as to carry out our God-given functions?

The three chapters in this section explore "form and function" in the hopes that this distinction might make a difference in the way we think about the church and the task of restoration. Chapter Four roots this distinction in Scripture. By defining these two concepts and then exploring how they are treated in the Bible (by the prophets, Paul, and Jesus), we discover a tool for getting at the core of our faith and the essence of our 'business' as the people of God. Chapter Five identifies the seven functions that have shaped the people of God throughout the Old and New Testaments. It calls us to "put the big rocks in first." Chapter Six addresses these functions in the context of the Restoration Movement. It suggests that we have often been guilty of confusing form and function, and even of ignoring vital functions entirely. And it argues that "faithfulness" involves the restoration of God's ancient functions, not the preservation of particular forms used to express them in times past.

Effective churches have a sense of purpose. They know why they exist.

Leif Anderson

4/ Form and Function: A Distinction that Matters

Consider the apple. Round and firm. Red (or green or yellow) skin. Stem poking out of one dimpled end. To examine an apple more closely, all that is needed is a paring knife. Cut through its diameter. Observe the white and moist flesh, seed pod holding brown and hardened orbs. By dissecting an apple in this way, it is possible to grasp the form of an apple—its *morphology*.

But there is more than one way to skin an apple, for there is more to this fruit than its form. Our understanding of *apple* is also determined by the *functions* it fulfills and the purposes it serves. An apple is part of the reproductive system of the apple tree: by means of the seed wrapped within this fruit, the tree propagates itself and its species. We make use of the apple for food: it is a featured ingredient in pies, pastries and other desserts, keeping the doctor (if not the dentist) away. Apples are traditionally used as gifts for teachers, to express affection and, one would suppose, curry favor. When rotten, the apple can be thrown to show disapproval.

Skinning the apple in this way requires a different kind of sharp instrument. It requires the "knife of logic," to use Robert Pirsig's memorable phrase.[1] By going beyond morphology to probe the utility of an apple, we are able to think past skin and flesh and stem to consider what functions this fruit performs. The knife of logic allows us to focus on questions of purpose, utility, and, ultimately, value.

Skinning the Church

The restoration plea has fallen victim to people wielding paring knives. They have dissected the ancient church down to its smallest components, creating along the way a *morphology* of God's people. They have described in detail how the first-century church was organized, the rituals and ceremonies it observed, the modes of its worship, the manner in which it operated. They have catalogued the role of evangelists, elders and deacons; the observance of the Supper; styles of singing, prayer and preaching; where the church met; how funds were collected and used; what ministries the church engaged in; what standards of morality were inculcated. And they have imagined that replicating those details in today's church is what restoration is all about.

Assuming for the moment that their observations about the early church have been accurate (an assumption I do not accept, as we will see in subsequent chapters), their great mistake has been in thinking that there is no other way to "skin" the ancient church. But there is much more to the church than its forms. Like the apple, the church has a functional aspect that must also inform our understanding of it. Having exhausted ourselves with measurement and definition and categorization, it yet remains for us to ask, "What was the mission of the New Testament church? What ends did it pursue? What purposes defined its identity and shaped its existence? What implications does all of that have for us?"

To answer such questions will require a different kind of sharp instrument than the one we have been using. We will need a logical knife that takes us past the morphology of the New Testament church to probe questions of purpose, utility, and value. But in that probing, I see promise of understanding better what the ancient church was about, and hope that the modern church can rediscover what it is we are to restore.

Toward a Definition of Form and Function

Definitions are rarely fun but often necessary. So grit your teeth and let's think more precisely about the meaning of *form* and *function* as these terms relate to the church.

By "form" I mean those methods, behaviors, and rituals through which the people of God give expression to their life under God—the *means* they use to carry out the spiritual business to which God has called them. By "function" I intend to denote the spiritual business itself—those *ends* that are definitional, fundamental, and central to our identity as God's people. "Function" addresses mission; "form" has to do with methodology. "Function" is about purpose; "form" addresses the means by which purpose is accomplished. "Function" asks *what*; "form" asks *how*. "Function" is concerned about which mountains we climb; "form" wonders by which route we should travel.

My dictionary defines *function* as the "duty, occupation, or role of a person," while one of the definitions listed for *form* is "procedure." That captures the distinction nicely. Functions have to do with "big picture" items on the church's plate—the "roles" God's people are called to fulfill. They define the reasons why we exist and the uses to which God puts us. Forms, on the other hand, describe the "pragmatics" in which the people of God engage—the tasks and "procedures" by which the church carries out its roles. Forms are the tangible methods by which the church conducts its mission.

As an example, you will soon read that I consider worship to be a primary function of God's people. Whether we talk about the Patriarchs, Moses, or the church—people who claim to be in relationship with God are always called to worship him. In particular, Christians have a responsibility to magnify, adore, and praise their Father and Savior—it is part of our God-given "business." *Whether* we should be a worshipping people is not debatable. It is one of the necessary "roles" to which we have been called.

How we are to worship, on the other hand, is open to much debate and variation. By asking "how," we have stopped talking about function and entered a discussion of form. In Corinth, Paul encouraged the church to worship by having women cover their heads (1 Cor. 11:5), honoring the Lord's Supper by sharing food with those in need (1 Cor. 11:20ff), giving preference to prophecy over tongues in the assembly (1 Cor. 14, especially 23-25), and ensuring that their open and highly participatory services were conducted in an orderly fashion (1 Cor. 14: 26ff). These were some of the *forms* through which the Corinthian Christians gave expression to the "worship" *function*.

But there is more to the function of worship than the particular forms practiced at Corinth. Identifying and imitating Corinthian forms will not necessarily ensure that the modern church functions as a worshipping community (any more than crafting wings in the shape of a bird's will guarantee that you can fly). Indeed, the commitment of the modern church to worship in "spirit and in truth" may lead it to devise forms that would never have occurred to the ancient Corinthians.

The church needs forms—means, methods, mechanisms—in order to exhibit the functions to which God has called us. Just as words are required to articulate thoughts, so forms are necessary to accomplish function—they are the idiom in which we express religious purposes.

But to say that forms are necessary to function is not to say they are *synonymous*. The distinction between forms and functions in religious life, between the means for doing business and the essential business itself, is an important one. Failure to make such a distinction—to so confuse form and function that they become indistinguishable—is the source of much mischief in Churches of Christ today. Clarifying this distinction can lead us to new insights about the church and how it should conduct itself.

Biblical Distinctions between Form and Function

Though the words "function" and "form" do not occur together in Scripture to define the religious life of God's people, the distinction is very much in evidence.

Take, for example, the idea of "covenant" and "sign." When God made a covenant with Noah never to destroy the earth with water again, he set a sign in the heavens—a rainbow (Gen. 9:9-17). The same thing occurred when God established a covenant relationship with Abraham; he instituted a "sign of the covenant"—circumcision (Gen. 17:1-14). The Sabbath Day is also called a "sign," symbolizing the covenant God made with Israel (Ex. 31:12-17).

But the sign was not itself the covenant. It pointed to the covenant. It symbolized the covenant. It was the form God chose to signify a covenant with his people. But the sign always pointed beyond itself to the ways in which God and his people were to function. In the end, it was the covenant, not the sign, that was vital.

Form and Function in the Prophets

This same distinction becomes evident in the prophetic writings. Israel had a hard time telling the difference between form and function. In the course of time, animal sacrifice became synonymous with holy living. Praying in the temple was the same as behaving in righteous ways. Evidently, Israel had fooled herself into believing that, so long as she observed the *forms* of a godly people, actually *functioning* as a godly people was not required. (We'll say more about this in Chapters Seven and Eight.)

The prophets begged to differ. One of their most important tasks was to re-educate Israel to the difference between religious ceremony and righteous living, between the forms of religion and its true functions. To do that, they often played one against the other, minimizing temple and cultus and ceremony in order to emphasize justice, mercy and faithfulness.

"The multitude of your sacrifices— what are they to me?" says the LORD. "I have no pleasure in the blood of bulls and lambs and goats. When you come to appear before me, who has asked this of you, this trampling of my courts? Stop bringing meaningless offerings! Your incense is detestable to me. New Moons, Sabbaths and convocations—I cannot bear your evil assemblies…Your hands are full of blood; wash and make yourselves clean. Take your evil deeds out of my sight! Stop doing wrong, learn to do right!" (Isa. 1:10-17)

Rend your heart and not your garments. (Joel 2:13)

With what shall I come before the LORD and bow down before the exalted God? Shall I come before him with burnt offerings, with calves a year old? He has showed you, O man, what is good. And what does the LORD require of you? To act justly and to love mercy and to walk humbly with your God. (Micah 6:6, 8)

The Israelites had managed to blur the line between religious forms (temple worship and sacrifice) and a religious function (holy living). They had succeeded in making the former synonymous with the latter. They had become meticulous about means and careless about ends. For our present purposes, it is important to see not that the prophets condemned such confusion (we will come back to this point later), but that they made a clear distinction between the methods used to interact with God and the lifestyle lived in submission to him.[2]

You find the same kind of language in the writings of David ("You do not take pleasure in burnt offerings. The sacrifices of God are a broken spirit"–Ps. 51:17), Jeremiah ("Will you steal and murder, commit adultery and perjury…and then come and stand before me in this house, which bears my Name, and say, 'We are safe?'"–Jer. 7:9-10), and Hosea ("I desire mercy, not sacrifice, and acknowledgment of God rather than burnt offerings"—Hos. 6:6). Each of these writers makes it clear that there is a meaningful difference between the condition of a worshipper's heart and the methods he uses to express himself to God. Proper ceremony is no substitute for a yielded life.

Form and Function in Paul

This distinction was very much on Paul's mind. As someone who had once "put confidence in the flesh" only to throw it all away for the "surpassing greatness of knowing Christ Jesus" (Phil. 3:4-8), Paul felt he had already wasted too much of his life on peripheral issues while missing the core of relationship with God. He developed a ruthless instinct for that which was "of Christ" and that which was "rubbish" in comparison, expending a great deal of energy teaching others to differentiate between "the form of godliness" and "the power" of it (2 Tim. 3:5).

Plow through his writings and you will turn up any number of references to this distinction between the essential business of the people of God and the particular (and transitory) ways in which that business is conducted.

Take, for instance, when he speaks to the Colossians of "shadows" and "reality": "Therefore do not let anyone judge you by what you eat or drink, or with regard to a religious festival, a New Moon celebration or a Sabbath day. These are a shadow of the things that were to come; the reality, however, is found in Christ" (Col. 2:16-17). Here Paul points to religious forms (that are being urged on the Colossians by Jewish Christians), and distinguishes between them and the hard kernel of Christian faith. He recognizes a difference between religious behaviors (some of which were God-ordained) and the essence of religious life. Even in Old Testament times, such forms were a "shadow" of Christ. They themselves were not the point, but mere illustrations of the point. To focus on the shadow and miss the reality is (for Paul) the characteristic flaw of his ancestral people.

Paul makes the same distinction between form and function when he comments to the Romans on how to treat the weaker brother. What should they do about members of the church who have convictions about food laws and the observance of special days? Paul tells them not to judge each other. He reminds them to act out of love about such matters. But then he makes a pronouncement on the matter, indicating that (when all is said and done) there is a distinction to be made between what is central and peripheral in the kingdom. "For the kingdom of God is not a matter of eating and drinking, but of righteousness, peace and joy in the Holy Spirit" (Rom. 14:17).

To the Galatians, Paul (emphatically) makes the same distinction: "For in Christ Jesus neither circumcision nor uncircumcision has any value. The only thing that counts is faith expressing itself through love" (Gal. 5:6).

Here again, Paul recognizes a difference between the trappings of religion (the forms—food laws, special days, circumcision) and essential religious business (the functions—Christ-centeredness, righteousness, faith). For Paul, the ability to see this difference is the necessary starting place for determining proper conduct as a Christian.

Form and Function in the Teachings of Jesus

It is in the teachings of Jesus, however, that this distinction between form and function is most evident. When accused of failing to encourage fasting among his disciples, Jesus responded that the fermenting functions of the kingdom of God would need new forms to contain them. "No one pours new wine into old wineskins. If he does, the wine will burst the skins, and both the wine and the wineskins will be ruined. No, he pours new wine into new wineskins" (Mk. 2:22).

Notice that Jesus does not argue for a "wineskin-less" religion (a religion without forms). He simply states that (in time) forms harden and habituate. When that happens, such forms are no longer fit containers for the bubbling presence of the gospel. New wineskins (i.e., new forms) must be found to hold the essence of the kingdom.

According to the Gospel accounts, Jesus was consistently enraged by the Pharisees' tendency to cling to their forms at the expense of divinely mandated functions. Now it is true that the Gospels consistently represent the Pharisees in the bleakest light. Perhaps their portrayal of these religious figures is overly negative, colored by the polemics of another time (the time at which the Gospels were written, decades after the events they recount). Not all Pharisees were apprentices to the Devil (e.g., Nicodemus). But—at their worst—the Pharisees were capable of some shocking confusion over the relative importance of religious forms and functions.

They obsessed about food laws and what went into their stomachs when they should have paid more attention to what came out of their mouths and hearts (Mk. 7:1-23). They worried about proper etiquette on the Sabbath while ignoring God's demand that his people show mercy (Mt. 12:9-14). They dissected the Scriptures but missed entirely the living Word of God (Jn. 5:39-40). They went to the temple to boast of their righteousness yet returned home unrepentant and unforgiven (Lk. 18:9-14). They wrangled over marriage and divorce, temple worship, and handwashing—while missing the fundamental nature of God. They were deeply worried about entering Pilate's presence and becoming unclean for the Passover, but not at all concerned about falsely accusing and murdering the Son of God. Each instance was further evidence to Jesus that these men had placed the forms of religion above its functions.

When Jesus distinguished between what was inside a man and what was on the outside, he was addressing ideas very similar to function and form. He touched on this idea in settling the great "hand-washing controversy," insisting that uncleanness results not from dirty hands (failing to observe the "washing" form) but from a dirty heart (failing to understand the holiness function— Mt. 15:17-20). He decried using external "acts of righteousness" (giving, praying, and fasting) as a means of gaining glory from men, but divorcing those actions from their intended religious purposes (Mt. 6:1-18).

Most of the "woes" pronounced in Matthew 23 against the religious leaders of his day focused on this inclination to major in external forms and minor in the change of heart that is the essential business of true religion. The Pharisees preached a good message but would not practice it. They had the words right but missed the meaning (Mt 23:2-4). They were fastidious about the form that oaths took but quite careless about honoring their commitments (Mt 23:16-22). They were very concerned about external appearances but neglectful of the internal transformations the Law was intended to foster.

> Woe to you, teachers of the law and Pharisees, you hypocrites! You clean the outside of the cup and dish, but inside they are full of greed and self-indulgence. Blind Pharisee! First clean the inside of the cup and dish, and then the outside also will be clean. Woe to you, teachers of the law and Pharisees, you hypocrites! You are like whitewashed tombs, which look beautiful on the outside but on the inside are full of dead men's bones and everything unclean. In the same way, on the outside you appear to people as righteous but on the inside you are full of hypocrisy and wickedness. (Mt. 23:25-28)

Echoing the language of the prophets, Jesus included in these "woes" a statement that is, surely, his sharpest distinction between form and function: "You give a tenth of your spices—mint, dill and cummin. But you have neglected the more important matters of the law—justice, mercy and faithfulness" (Mt. 23:23).

Once again, Jesus draws a line between what is peripheral and what is central, between lesser matters and "the more important matters," between the forms we use to interact with God and the basic functions to which God has called us.

Whether Jesus is discussing wine and wineskins, commands and traditions, heart-worship and ceremony, the desire to please God and external acts, the inside and the outside, or faithfulness and tithing, he is making a consistent distinction between the functions of religion and its forms.

The Patriarchs. The Prophets. Paul. Jesus. The sources are many. The issues are diverse. The language is varied. But the message in all these biblical references is consistent. When it comes to religion and our life before God, there are principles and there are practices; there are ends and there are means. It is this distinction I am trying to get at by using the terms "form" and "function."

And Now, A Word From Our Sponsors

A restoration slogan hints to us of the same distinction: "Doing Bible things in Bible ways." "Bible things" suggests the same ends and purposes, the essential spiritual business, that I am calling "function." "Bible ways" alludes to the means and methods I have designated "form." Our movement has tended to focus on the latter, concluding that what was most needed for the church of our day was a closer scrutiny of *how* the early church attended to its business. So out came the paring knife to begin the meticulous dissection of church practices in Corinth, Rome, Ephesus, etc.

Perhaps we took for granted that we understood what "Bible things" are called for, that we grasped fully the business they (and we) should be about. Perhaps we thought such issues to be so basic as to need no comparable and careful study. Or, perhaps, we so completely confused form and function that we failed to note any difference between "things" and "ways"—and, thus, failed to draw a distinction that could have made a real difference for us.

The result is that we have never found, hardly even looked for, that logical knife which would allow us to probe the New Testament church for signs of its purpose and function. We can tell you how often early churches took the Supper, whether they cooperated with other congregations in benevolence and mission efforts, what role deacons played, and why they did not have basketball hoops in their multi-purpose auditoriums. But sit us down and ask us to tell you not what they did but who they were, what they valued, the purposes that drove them, the goals they pursued—and we are likely to give you a blank stare.

Yet there is a great deal to learn about this aspect of church life. For it is precisely the issue of function in the New Testament church that bears greatest promise for teaching us who they were and who we, today, are meant to be. In fact, as I will suggest, it is the focus on function that can breathe new life into the restoration plea. We need to be busy restoring the New Testament church. But not the ways in which it conducted business. We need to restore the business itself.

Quite simply, the criterion of biblical validity means that all church structures should in fact help the Church be the Church and carry out its mission. They should be structures which promote community, build disciples and sustain witness. Structures which in fact do this are valid; structures which do not are invalid, regardless of how aesthetic, efficient or venerated they may be.

Howard Snyder

5/ The Seven Functions of God's People

In a recent book on time management,[1] the author told of a demonstration that made an indelible impression. During a seminar, the speaker pulled a wide-mouthed jar and a platter of fist-sized rocks from behind his podium. "How many of these rocks do you think we can get in this jar?" The audience made several guesses, after which the lecturer placed one rock after another into the container—right up to the rim.

"Is the jar full now?" he asked. Everyone agreed that is was—until the lecturer pulled out a bag of gravel and began pouring it around the rocks, filling up the crevices between. Smiling, he asked, "Now is the jar full?" This time, the audience was more cautious. The speaker brought out a pitcher of water and poured its contents into the jar.

"Now," he said, addressing his audience intently. "What is the point of this little demonstration?" As this was a seminar on time management, one participant gave the predictable response: "No matter how busy you are, there is always room to fit more into your life."

"No," said the speaker. "That's not the point. The point is: You've got to put the big rocks in first."

Defining the Church

In a Wednesday night class recently, I asked a group of college students to name the 'marks' of the true church. They quickly rattled off a long list: taking the Supper weekly, acapella singing, autonomous congregations, elders and deacons, supporting poor college students (actually, they made up that last one).

Then I asked them to state the essential *business* of God's kingdom, the fundamental work God has called his people to accomplish. They looked at me for a while, not understanding the question. I tried again. "What is the church *for*? Why are we here? What is God trying to *do* through us?" Once more they stared, turning the words over in their minds, trying to fit the question to an answer they knew. "To restore the New Testament church?" one of the students hesitantly asked.

I decided to give them a hint. "Do you believe the church exists to reach out to lost people and tell them the good news about Jesus?" Oh, yes! They believed that. They knew evangelism should be a priority for the church. "So, why else does the church exist? What other purposes has God decreed for the church?" They pondered and squirmed and worried. Over the next few minutes, they managed to identify two (worship and service) of the seven functions that—to me—summarize the essential business of God's people.

After class, several of the students approached me with similar comments. "That was hard. I've never thought about the church in that way. Seems like I should be able to identify the core purposes of the church. But when you asked us to name them, I drew a blank."

That, in microcosm, is the problem. We are a people focused on means, not ends. We obsess over the route, but pay scant attention to the destination. We have defined ourselves by the practices of the New Testament church. (Pour that gravel into the jar!) We have defined ourselves by our distinctives—how we differ from the churches around us. (Now, pour in the water!) But, too often, we have failed to put the big rocks in first. There is little room left in our understanding of the church for those purposes that comprise the essential business of God's people.

What would a definition of the church—one that put the big rocks in first—look like? When you boil the people of God down to their essentials, what big themes emerge? These are the functions God calls his people to pursue, the goals God asks us to attempt. By focusing on those functions, we ensure that the big rocks go in first as we construct our understanding of who the church is and what the church does.

Back to Basics

As we think about our understanding of the church, let's ask a different kind of question than the one we usually ask. Instead of looking at the first-century church and inquiring, "*How* did these people do business? What forms did they use?" let's question, "*What* business did these people do, and *why*? What functions did they perform?" This small change in syntax skews our focus away from the *practices* of God's people toward the *goals* and *purposes* they pursued. By beginning with these "ends" in mind, we are immediately required to pay attention to matters that, by definition, are at the core of our life together. We are forced to think about the big rocks.

What exactly is the business of the kingdom of God? What goals and ambitions should God's people embrace? What purposes are central to our existence? To use the language of the last chapter, what "covenant" has God struck with those who would be his people, what "more important matters" has he commissioned us to perform? What are the "realities," the "things that count," the "new wine" that shape the life of the people of God?

In what follows, I name seven functions that Scripture attests for the ancient church.[2] As we will see, these functions hold not just for the first-century church but for every manifestation of God's people across time and circumstance. There has always been a core of religious purposes for which God's people, in every age, have been responsible. Certainly, there are differences in the particular forms used to address those functions during the Patriarchal, Mosaic, and Christian dispensations. But there are also many and profound similarities among the functions God has always called his people to fulfill. While the forms may vary, the functions remain the same. They are eternal. Immutable. Fixed.

The Seven Functions

Worship. Holiness. Community. Maturation. Service. Witness. Influence.

These seven words summarize the work God has entrusted to his church. They represent areas of responsibility, purposes to pursue, that transcend time and culture and circumstance. These are the ideals that define the church of Jesus Christ. These are the big rocks that must go in first.

Unlike rocks, however, these categories are not discrete. There is a great deal of overlap between them. They spill over and leak into one another. Each builds and depends on the others. Each informs and supplements the others. How can a church worship effectively, for instance, without also having a hunger for holiness or a commitment to loving each other? How can a church effectively witness without a commitment to serve the lost and mature its converts?

Yet each function describes a sphere of activity so important, so necessary to the life of the church, that it deserves separate treatment. To leave one out is to impoverish the experience of the church and ignore a mandate from the church's head. God wants his people to function in all these areas. There are no options here. You cannot take some and leave the rest. A healthy church will be concerned to address each function thoughtfully, creatively and effectively.

The first two functions remind us that we are called to live vertically. The church reaches up through worship and holy living to commune with God. In worship, we adore him. In holiness, we dedicate our lives to him.

1. God's people are called to worship.

Worship is, arguably, the primary function of God's people. By the fourth chapter of Genesis, Cain and Abel were building altars and making sacrifices. Worship was the first thing Noah did upon embarking from the ark. Worship was a regular part of Abraham's routine. It is not unusual, in reading through Genesis, to find a patriarch pausing to build an altar and offering up grateful homage to God.

Under Moses, the first two of the Ten Commandments spoke to the centrality of worshipping God, and him alone. The most formative events of Israel's history[3] were punctuated by outpourings of public worship. The Old Testament canon contains entire books devoted to or written in the context of worship.[4]

Clearly, New Testament churches were worshipping communities. Individually, Christians were taught to cultivate an attitude and lifestyle of worship. They were expected to live worshipful lives and to glorify God in all their actions. Corporately, they gathered regularly to offer up praise and devotion to God. The New Testament bears ample testimony to the special sanctity and importance of worship by the assembled church.[5]

But biblical worship should never be confused with assemblies or rituals or behaviors. Worship in Scripture is an experience of the presence of God. It calls God's people to think on God, to consider his mighty acts, to contemplate his character. It invites men and women of faith to express brokenness, gratitude, awe, joy, fear, and humility before God. True worship calls forth a language of the heart that may involve words, is often expressed with words, but ultimately transcends words.[6]

Worship can occur in a closet or a church building. In fact, it needs to occur in both. A regular recognition of the vertical dimension of our lives—so foreign to the flat and spiritually-oblivious world in which we moderns exist—is a key function for the people of God. God wants his church to look up. He demands regular, emotive, God-honoring and life-changing worship whereby we acknowledge that God is on his throne and we are at his feet.

You cannot build a church that flies without a foundation of worship.

2. God's people are called to be holy.

Holiness flows from effective worship. You do not experience God's presence, you cannot express adoration and praise, without developing a desire to be like him. In worship, we commune with God. In holiness, we live out his life.

The invitation to become God's people has always been coupled with a demand for holiness. For every "Come to me" there is a "Come out and be separate." The Israelites were forbidden to imitate the lifestyles of their neighbors. Instead, they were required to "Be holy, because I am holy" (Lev. 11:45). Christians in Corinth or Rome were called to rise above the shabby morality of their cultures. Paul exhorted his churches "to be holy" and to "live a holy life" (1 Cor. 1:2; 1 Thess. 4:7).

It is easy to confuse holiness with ethical living, doing the right things, avoiding sin. But holiness is bigger than that. Holiness involves developing a taste for God, a hunger for righteousness. It involves the notion of separating ourselves for—dedicating ourselves to—godly living. It implies an active pursuit motivated by a passion for God and a revulsion of the sinful and profane. Holiness can be glimpsed in Phinehas' zeal for God (Num. 25:10-13), David's "panting" for God (Ps. 42:1), Paul's consuming dedication to the Christ of the gospel (Phil. 3:7-11).

It is also easy to confuse holiness with the adoption of particular religious forms. Circumcision, observance of food laws, and even manner of dress were ways in which the Israelites demonstrated their commitment to holiness. There can be no true holiness without a measure of distinctiveness (even peculiarity) in the way we act, think and live. But holiness is not synonymous with particular forms. The forms change and adapt with changes in culture and circumstance. What remains constant is the persistent call for God's people to carefully, thoughtfully, relevantly swim against the tide of profane culture.

Once again, holiness must be expressed personally and corporately. In both Testaments, individuals are called to walk like God, to hunger for him and shape their lives around him. And, in both Testaments, the community of faith is charged with encouraging holiness, rewarding holiness, and protecting itself against the encroachments of an unholy world.

When God's people take holiness seriously, we please our holy God and open ourselves to his blessings. When we grow casual about holiness, we demonstrate through careless living a careless disregard for him.

You cannot build a church that flies without a passionate pursuit of holiness.

The third and fourth functions remind us that we are also called to live horizontally. The church relates to itself by building intimate community and fostering Christ-like maturity. Through community, we demonstrate our love for each other. By growing each other up in Christ, we ensure that strong disciples and strong churches are developed.

3. God's people are called to be a community.
God has always been interested in building intimate communities. As soon as he calls an individual into relationship with himself, God introduces that person into a society of like-minded others.

Through Abraham, God built a clan. Through Moses, he built a nation. Through Jesus and the apostles, he built a church. But God is not the only one "building" his communities of faith. Those he calls also have a role to play in supporting this communal aspect of their experience before God. We, too, are in the business of building groups.

There is an "ethic of community" that must pervade our understanding of what it means to be God's people. God has called us into an extended family. We are bound together by common faith and common blood. We are commanded to love each other, live in harmony together, forgive, encourage and serve, lay down our lives for each other, share our possessions.[7] We belong to each other in many and profound ways.[8]

In a world characterized by loneliness, isolation, and self-centeredness, God's people provide a striking contrast. At least they should. Certainly, the family of God has had its share of family struggles: Jacob and Esau, Joseph and his brothers, the squabbling Israelites, the Corinthian church, Euodia and Syntyche. Those struggles continue today. God's people have always found the call to community a difficult summons to obey.

But if, through the ages, God's people did not always act like a community, they certainly knew how God expected them to function. The pursuit of an intimate, inclusive and unified fellowship has been a consistent characteristic of those who are in relationship with God. Though different forms have been adopted through the centuries to express that fellowship, the underlying notion that "we who are many form one body, and each member belongs to all the others" (Rom. 12:5) is a constant refrain for God's chosen people.

You cannot build a church that flies without the component of community.

4. God's people are called to mature each other.

Making disciples is a critical function of God's people. I don't mean making converts. And I don't mean making clueless clones of ourselves. I do mean the intentional, deliberate, methodical process of growing people into spiritual maturity. I do mean raising up people who are trained and equipped for life in the kingdom.

In the Old Testament, this mandate often involved raising children "in the way they should go." Fathers were told to teach God's commandments to their children, to tell the story of God's mighty acts to their sons and daughters, and to show by their own lives the path their offspring should follow. The entire book of

Proverbs demonstrates a father's concern to shape the mind and life of his son.

Indeed, some of the saddest chapters of Israel's history chronicle what happened when this function was ignored. The downward spiral of Judges ("Another generation grew up, who knew neither the LORD nor what he had done for Israel," Judg. 2:10), the tragic failure of Eli ("Your sons do not walk in your ways," 1 Sam. 8:5), and the tendency of good kings to have rotten children (e.g., David and Absalom) attest to the fact that, too often, Israel did not effectively teach its children, and paid a terrible price as a result.

But, even in the Old Testament, this shaping was not limited to parents and children. The apprenticeship of Samuel under Eli, Moses' mentoring of Joshua, the partnership of Elijah and Elisha, and Mordechi's relationship with Esther bear testimony to the importance of mature, spiritual people training and guiding the leadership of tomorrow.

In New Testament times, the emphasis shifted from biological to spiritual offspring. These first Christians recognized there was more to following Jesus than simply hearing and making an initial response to the story of the cross. And so we read letters written to teach new Christians how to develop as disciples. We see strong and lasting relationships (mentoring relationships) established between older leaders and younger co-workers—Paul and Timothy, Barnabas and John Mark, John and Gaius. We hear the apostles urging their converts to devote themselves to Scripture and to let the "word of Christ" dwell in them. We listen over the centuries as less mature disciples are told to "grow up" into Christ and to be "conformed" to his image (Eph. 4:15; Rom. 8:29).

There has always been a discipling function incumbent on the people of God. When the church attends to that business, people are constantly being grown into the image of Christ, and the future of God's community is protected. When this function is ignored, God's people will struggle and falter. Apostasy, as they say, is only a generation away.

You cannot build a church that flies without a commitment to raising mature disciples.

The final three functions remind us that we are called to live in the world and for the world. Christians reach out through service, witness and influence to a world that needs what we have to offer. Through service, we minister to the world's hurts. Through witness, we testify to the world's Savior. And through being salt and light, we dare to make a difference in this present darkness.

5. God's people are called to serve.

The story of Abraham is not the story of a man in isolated communion with God and his family. It is the story of a man who was concerned about and eager to serve the people around him. Abraham went to war to protect the people he lived among and offered hospitality to strangers. He begged God to spare Sodom, and played the role of peacemaker with his neighbors.

Under the law of Moses, Israel was required to attend to the needs of others. God told his people to minister to widows and orphans, and to the "aliens" living among them. Under the law, concern for the poor, compassion, and acts of mercy were as important as sacrifice—more so, in some cases (Hos. 6:6; Mic. 6:6-8; Zech. 7:4ff). Whole classes of people in Israel—the priests, Levites, and prophets—dedicated themselves to the service of God and others. Ruth is commended in Scripture for her tender ministries to her mother-in-law.

But it is in the New Testament that the ethic of ministry finds its highest expression. Jesus roots his own purpose (and that of his disciples) in the call not "to be served, but to serve." His example of self-sacrifice, concern for others, and eagerness to minister to both friend and stranger…his teachings on the "greatest in the kingdom" and the need to "wash one another's feet"… these shaped an essential function for the church.

Though ministry has taken different forms through the centuries (rarely are we moderns called to wash each other's feet), God has always expected his people to be a compassionate people, to care for the needs of others, and to pour themselves out in service. When we engage in selfless ministry, we partake in both the nature and the work of our Lord.

You cannot build a church that flies without a commitment to meaningful ministry.

6. God's people are called to witness.

God has always asked his people to serve an evangelistic function in the world. In the days of the patriarchs, this mandate primarily involved physical reproduction. "Go forth and multiply" was God's way of telling his ancient peoples that they had a responsibility to grow His kingdom numerically. Even so, Israel still testified to the surrounding nations of God's goodness. Jonah's reluctant ministry to Ninevah, the Jewish slave girl who testified so eagerly to Naaman, and Daniel's impact on Nebuchadnezzar are a few examples of ancient Israelites "evangelizing" their world. We read regularly of proselytes, converts and "God-fearers"—Gentiles who came to believe in Yahweh because of the witness of the Jewish people.

By the time of the church, however, the mandate to grow the kingdom was primarily a matter of spiritual reproduction. Teaching, rather than procreation, became the basis upon which the New Testament church expanded. Jesus (who defined his own ministry in terms of "seeking and saving the lost") commissioned his followers to go, preach and make disciples. The numerical growth of the early church is a testament to the pervasiveness and effectiveness of its witness. It wasn't just the message of these early Christians that turned the world upside down—it was their persistent proclamation of it.

Of course, not all New Testament churches were equally competent in their evangelistic outreach. Antioch was the most ardently missionary church. Jerusalem Christians, finally and under compulsion, went everywhere "preaching the word" (Acts 8:4). The Corinthians are known for many things, but not necessarily for their enthusiasm in sharing the gospel with others.

However we might grade their effectiveness, it is clear they had all heard the command to "Go!" They knew that an important function of God's people was to vigorously testify to the life, death and resurrection of Jesus. If they didn't always excel at this, they at least knew enough to hang their heads when confronted with a lack of evangelistic fruit.

Evangelistic witness has always been characteristic of those who are in relationship with God. Though different means and methods have been employed through the centuries to tell of God's greatness and move outsiders to faith, the function of witness is a constant for the people of God.

You cannot build a church that flies without a deep commitment to sharing good news.

7. God's people are called to influence their world.

There is one more function God's people fulfill in their interaction with the world. Yes, they serve others. And, yes, they share faith. But the people of God also have a responsibility to share their lifestyle and elevate the morals of the surrounding culture through example, confrontation, and teaching. Sometimes our contact with the world has little to do with bringing people to faith, or alleviating needs, and much to do with making life in the world more palatable.

On occasion, ancient Israel exercised this influence by wiping out pockets of depravity—elevating the morals of her world by eliminating immoral cultures. (What God did at Sodom, he asked Israel to do with the people of Canaan, for instance, Deut. 7:1-2.) At other times, however, Israel's influence was less militant. She was intended to be a "light to the nations," shaming surrounding cultures by confronting low living with a higher righteousness. (The influence of Daniel and his friends on the eating habits of the Babylonians is but one example, Dan. 1:6-16.)

By the first century, Jesus was anticipating a church that would be leaven in a sin-flattened culture. He called his disciples the "salt of the earth" and the "light of the world." As they lived in the world, Christ's followers were intended to have an elevating effect on their neighbors.

This can happen fortuitously when the church provides a compelling example of true community and holiness for a world that has lost all sense of fraternity and morality. It certainly happens when, one by one, people of the world are adopted into the family of God. But there is an *intentional* aspect of being "salt" and "light" involved here as well. The church of the first century deliberately, programmatically impinged on the cultures that surrounded it— just as Jesus their Lord did.

The story is told, for example, of Christians who gathered at the *lactaria* on the outskirts of Rome at dusk. They would watch furtive figures from the town deposit small bundles—unwanted children (often female or deformed) who would be left to the elements or wild beasts. The Christians would rescue these infants and raise them as their own sons and daughters. The church had an important role to play in shaming popular culture into abandoning such practices.[9]

The role of the early church in providing for widows and orphans, the poor and sick, the unwanted of society had a major impact on the attitudes and habits of the culture at large. Building hospitals, emancipating slaves, elevating perspectives on women, encouraging mutuality in marriage, redefining leadership ethics— in these and a hundred other ways, the kingdom of God has salted the kingdom of men.

This kind of influence has always been characteristic of those who are in relationship with God. Though that influence has taken different forms through the centuries, God's people have tried to make a difference in the flavor of their world. Being salt has been a consistent function for the people of God over time and across cultures.

You cannot build a church that flies without the commitment to be salt and light.

Conclusion

These, then, are the seven components that are essential to building a functioning church. They hold true for every manifestation of God's people across time and circumstance. They comprise the core of religious purposes for which God's people, in every age, are responsible.

When a church today pursues effective worship, holy living, intimate community, intentional maturation, sacrificial service, powerful witness, and substantive influence, it is pursuing the essential business of the kingdom. We can argue over means and methods. We can debate the forms. But these are the irreducible functions of God's people. Get these right and a church cannot go far wrong, whatever means and methods it uses.

The beauty of focusing on functions rather than forms—of asking "what" instead of "how"—is that we are permitted to pay attention to the big rocks. We can think about "weightier matters" rather than drowning in a sea of details. Instead of obsessing with ladder-climbing techniques, we can ensure our ladder is leaning against the right wall.

By looking at functions, we have the chance to adjust our understanding of what church is about, and focus once again on what is most important.

That is a necessary step for those of us who are members of Churches of Christ. Many of us have immersed ourselves for so long in the complexities of doing church—in the details and minutia of religious practice—we have forgotten the basic themes that give coherence to what we do. To beat the airplane metaphor to death— we've been so focused on individual rivets, we have forgotten about the essential shape of the wing.

Indeed, as the next chapter demonstrates, those of us whose roots run deep in the Restoration Movement may well have come to a point where we deny there is a wing. Getting the rivets right is all that matters. The forms have become our function. The means have become our end. How we do business has become synonymous for us with the business God has called us to do.

How sad. Such a mindset is almost guaranteed to keep us from putting the big rocks in first. Our definition of the church will be full to the rim with details and particulars and specifics—the gravel and water of church life. But when asked, "What are our purposes? What is God trying to accomplish through us?" we may realize we have no answer that fits such questions.

All things that resist

change are changed by

that resistance in ways

undesired and undesirable.

Gary Wills

6/ Building a Functional Church

The dominant approach our heritage has taken with the ancient church has been *descriptive*. We measured and defined and catalogued. We noted how early churches behaved during worship, how they encouraged fellowship and holiness, how they practiced evangelism and ministry.

These snapshots of first-century Christianity added up to a pattern (indeed, *the* pattern) that "faithful" Christians would carry over the centuries and apply to the church today. We assumed that restoration was a matter of behaving now as they did then, shaping ourselves by their ancient example. If only we could reproduce their forms, we could become a faithful church.

But in our determination to describe the ancient church's forms, we hardly paused to ponder its spiritual functions. We asked "how" but rarely pushed on to wonder "what" and "why." It is time for us to wonder that now. Faithfulness requires more of us than replicating ancient forms—reusing the containers that held their worship and carried their witness and shaped their communities. Instead, our focus must shift to the contents themselves—that divine and vital business that motivated the ancient church and needs to animate us.

In the last chapter, I identified seven functions that must shape the people of God: Worship. Holiness. Community. Maturity. Service. Witness. Influence. Seven answers to the question, "What is the essential business of God's people?" Seven big rocks to place in the jar of God's church. How have the people of God addressed these functions throughout history? In different ways. Our concern at present, however, is not to ask "how" but to establish the "what"—to trace the foundational outlines of the work God has given us to do. This chapter continues that effort, with specific application to Churches of Christ.

But I hope to do more in the following paragraphs. I want to introduce the "Why" question more fully—to explore whether any clarity results from understanding better why these functions are so central to the business of the church.

The answer to the "Why" question begins with a return to the incarnation theme. The church exists to incarnate Jesus Christ—to become his presence, in reality and substance, within this world. First and foremost, the seven functions we've talked about take their significance not from our ability to document them in the actions of Abraham or Moses or Paul—the church of Israel or the church of the New Testament—but from the fact that we see these functions alive and active in the life of our Lord. Jesus demonstrated his commitment to these functions. Since we take our shape from him, we also must make these functions our business.

Why does the church worship? Because Christ did. Why are we concerned with holiness and intimate community and building Christ-like lives in others? Because we see our model engaged in these activities. Why should we bother with service and witness and influencing the world? Because Jesus bothered with them.

But there is more. Push the incarnation theme very hard, and you run into Christ's Father and Christ's Spirit. You recognize that the functions so characteristic of Jesus are also fundamental to the activity of God and the Comforter. You discover that the business of the church is rooted in the work of the Trinity, that we participate in their activity when we pursue these same goals.

Dip these seven functions into the Trinity and they come up dripping with new meanings and fresh importance. Why does the church pursue holiness and witness to a lost world and build intimate community? Because we long to participate in the life and work of God the Father, God the Son, and God the Spirit.

Before launching into the rest of this chapter, it remains for me to spell out two radical implications of what we've just discussed. The first is that God/Son/Spirit have more than a past tense relationship with the business of the kingdom. They are presently and fully engaged in the pursuit of these functions. As we will see, the challenge for the church, then, is not to engage in religious business for God/Son/Spirit but to join and participate with them in the spiritual work that is currently taking place in the heavenly realms.

The second implication is even more critical. Since kingdom business remains God's business, since the church participates in (rather than taking over) that business, divine power is still the fundamental fuel of the kingdom. We do not empower the kingdom by our discipline and correctness and proper enactment of particular religious forms. The church is a vessel into which the power of God is poured in order to accomplish his work. Where the church is concerned (and in contrast to the usual interpretation of the Parable of the Talents), God has not gone away, leaving us to invest our talents as best we can, only to return after a long while to demand an accounting. God, his Son, and his Spirit are vitally involved with and a present source of power for the work we have been called to do.

Does this all sound mystical and abstract? Perhaps what follows will convince you otherwise.

God's People are called to Worship

Who will not fear you, O Lord, and bring glory to your name? For you alone are holy. All nations will come and worship before you, for your righteous acts have been revealed. (Rev. 15:4)

When we ask, "What was worship to the first Christians? Why did they worship?" rather than, "How did they conduct their worship?" we get a different kind of answer than we have come to expect. Rather than discussing style of singing and frequency of meeting and order of service, we find ourselves reflecting on the function of worship for first-century Christians.

Worship was not just an event for early Christians—it was an experience. It transported them to a "holy place" where they met with their Lord and experienced his power (1 Cor. 5:4; 2 Cor. 12:2-4). It allowed them to participate in the ongoing worship of Christ, their High Priest (Heb. 4:14-5:10). Empowered by the Spirit, worship was a convicting, humbling, awe-inducing activity in which Christians bowed down and acknowledged that God was present with them (1 Cor. 14:24-25).[1] It produced in them a vivid awareness of their own sin and unworthiness, and a compelling urge to praise, adore and testify to God's greatness. Whether spontaneous or structured, mediated through an apostle or conducted in a catacomb, involving song or teaching or ecstatic utterances, worship provided a vibrant connection between these believers and their God.

But that is not how we have envisioned our worship. Our focus has been on the "how" of worship, not the "what." We've traced through our Bibles to find behaviors in which the first churches engaged when gathered for worship. We've identified five "acts"—preaching, singing, praying, the Supper, and giving—that are connected in some way with the early church's behavior during assembled worship.[2]

And, in a monumental confusion of form and function, we've imagined that true worship occurs when those particular forms are enacted. If the church engages in the "five acts," then worship has happened—whether or not there is any experience of God or trembling in his presence or conviction of sin. We reduce worship to executing the right elements in the right order on the right day.

"Proper" worship forms become synonymous with (indeed, identical to) functioning as a worshipful people.

But what about the healing, joyous, adoring, convicting, penitential function that worship served for first-century Christians? What about worship as an opportunity to participate in heavenly devotions, to be caught up in the Spirit on the Lord's Day, to be "lost in wonder, love and praise"? Shouldn't we, as restoration people, be concerned to restore these things?

There may have been a time when we were content to measure ourselves by how correctly we reproduced first-century forms of worship. But no longer. We are hungry for an experience of worship in which God becomes present with us, his goodness is praised and honored, and his people are humbled and strengthened. It is the restoration of worship function, not the reproduction of worship forms, that should be the true goal of people who want to build a faithful church.

> We must ask ourselves whether our forms of worship convey the gospel. Do they help people to apprehend the worship and ministry of Christ as he draws us by the Spirit into a life of shared communion, or do they hinder? Do they make the real presence of Christ transparent in worship, or do they obscure it? To answer these questions, we have to look at the meaning, the content of worship, before we can decide whether our traditions and procedures are adequate. More profoundly, we have to consider our doctrine of God in worship. Is he the triune God of grace who has created us and redeemed us to participate freely in his life of communion and in his concerns for the world or is he the contract-God who has to be conditioned into being gracious by what we do—by our religion?"[3]

If fresh forms will encourage in our people a renewed sense of the presence of God, we should explore those new forms so that we can be faithful to old functions. Clinging to old worship forms that have ceased calling us to a transforming experience of God is not "faithfulness." Indeed, it represents a greater threat to the church than the worship "innovations" we have been taught to fear.

God's People are Called to be Holy

> As obedient children, do not conform to the evil desires you had when you lived in ignorance. But just as he who called you is holy, so be holy in all you do. (1 Pet. 1:14-15)

It is easy to see *how* the first Christians practiced the call to holiness. Paul described what holiness should look like in Corinth and Ephesus and Rome. He included specific and practical portraits of ethical Christian living in most of his epistles.

But in Paul's mind, holiness would never be achieved through simply codifying Christian ethics.[4] Real holiness involved more than correct behavior. (Consider the Pharisees!) Somehow, these early Christians had to catch a hunger for holiness. They had to develop a passion for living in a way that pleased the Lord (Col. 1:10).

When we ask not *how* the early church expressed holiness but *what* holiness meant for them and *why* they put such emphasis on it, we have to think about holiness differently. Holiness is a core characteristic of God himself. It was demonstrated tangibly in the earthly life of Christ. It is at the heart of the transformative work being done within us by the Spirit. When Christians pursue holiness, they participate in the nature of God, in the walk of Jesus, and in the ongoing endeavors of the Holy Spirit.

Within this framework, it is easy to see why Paul placed such emphasis on the matter of holiness—and how we cheapen holiness by reducing it to rules for moral living or the observance of specific religious forms. Paul was not interested in simply elevating his readers' behavior. He wanted to elevate their thinking. He wanted them to fall in love with a different level of existence, a life in "the Spirit" rather than in "the flesh." His readers were urged to live "worthy of the gospel of Christ," to be "imitators of God," to "shine like stars," to set their hearts and minds "on things above."[5] Holiness was not a matter of rule-keeping but of understanding how to "put on the new man," to become "slaves to righteousness," and to "know Christ."[6]

Though Paul made lists of vices to avoid and virtues to attain, conformity to lists was never his aim. Conformity to Christ was his goal. Shouldn't we, as restoration people, share that goal?

And, to some extent, we do. We recognize the need to be *separate* from our world, to live out a higher morality. We appeal to the life of Jesus to inculcate behaviors and attitudes that should be characteristic of God's people. We do want to "live worthy" of our high calling.

At the same time, however, let's confess that we have been drawn more to holiness forms than to holiness functions. It has been easier for us to enforce ethical rules than to develop people who hungered for righteousness. As a practical matter, we've valued conformity above virtue. A focus on "drinking, dancing, and smoking," has been substituted for a clarion call to "be transformed by the renewing of your mind" (Rom. 12:2). Too often, we have opted to do morality by rote.

In a word, the temptation Paul avoided became the policy we often pursued. We formulated virtue and vice lists (some items drawn from the New Testament, but many more drawn from the moralisms popular in rural America around the turn of the last century).[7] We constructed a binding (if unwritten) moral creed. And we relied on peer pressure or church disciplinary action to enforce that creed on our members.

Those who are interested in restoring not just the "form of godliness" but the "power of it" understand that holiness works from the inside out. They know Christian purity involves something besides the avoidance of certain vices or the incorporation of certain virtues. They realize that holiness is produced not by inculcating rules but by an indwelling Spirit whose power is at work within God's people. They are eager to point to a spiritual dynamic for holiness that far transcends the morality-by-the-numbers being dispensed from some of our pulpits and lecterns.

Grasping how true holiness functions will allow us to emphasize character rather than codes. It will encourage questions about morality rather than squelching moral debate. It will promote education that aims for ethical thinking rather than Pavlovian responses. It will permit us to distinguish between those matters that are central to holy living and those that have more to do with culture and personal preference. It will hold up Christ-likeness as the goal of Christian living. It will stress God's work within us more than our need to work harder.

As our world grows more profane, the church cannot afford to settle for an anemic holiness measured by superficial standards. We must call our people to eager confession, deep repentance, Christ-modeled lives, and godly thoughts. We must encourage each other to be so ravenous for righteousness that we will not allow pride or discomfort or embarrassment to keep us from the feast. If fresh approaches to holiness will encourage our people to keep their eyes on Jesus and walk more closely in his steps, we should explore those new forms so we can be faithful to the holiness function.

God's People are Called to be a Community

As I have loved you, so you must love one another. (Jn. 13:34)

Christian community is a reflection of the perfect community God enjoys with his Son and his Holy Spirit. The dynamics of their relationship—the intimacy and self-giving that characterize life in the Trinity—become the goal and standard of the community we enjoy in the church. Our community is not primarily an obedient response to relational commands. Far less is it a tool we manipulate to enforce conformity and protect orthodoxy. It is, rather, a participation—here and now—in the fellowship enjoyed—there and forever—by those in the heavenly realms.

Why did the early Christians value and embrace the community of God's people? Because they believed that such a radical community would honor the heavenly community and demonstrate God's power to a watching world.

Now it is true that the apostles talked about organizational matters such as leadership and "fellowship" boundaries and love feasts in their teachings about the community of faith. But the significant issues about Christian community had little to do with particular forms. The apostles wanted to build functional fellowships. They called the early church to be an environment where lonely, selfish, stubborn, opinionated, headstrong, bitter, and unloving people were taught to become more like their Master. They expected Christians to take off a life-time of bad relational habits and put on a "new self" characterized by tolerance, kindness, gentleness, and forgiveness. They taught a new "ethic for relationships" characterized by mutual submission, deferring to one another, putting others' needs first, accepting the weaker brother, refraining from judgment, building each other up, forgiving, protecting unity and peace, shunning division, honoring the least, getting rid of complaining and grumbling and unwholesome talk, serving each other out of love. They intended that the church community reflect and incarnate the intimate relationship of the Trinity and the heavenly hosts.

Unfortunately, that is not how we have thought about community. These are not the categories that have channeled our exploration of God's family. Rather than pursuing New Testament intimacy in our churches, we focused on imitating New Testament structures. We analyzed organizational models (elders and deacons), forums for interaction (corporate assemblies and fellowship meals, rented halls and homes), names the first churches went by, the roles of evangelists, and how one church related to another. We studied the proper ways to "extend" fellowship and "limit" fellowship and "refuse" fellowship and "withdraw" fellowship.

But what about the loving, sharing, training, encouraging, correcting intimacy of first-century fellowship? What about the first church's desire to reflect on earth an intimacy born in heaven? As restoration people, shouldn't we be passionate about restoring that?

Sometimes, it seems we've run right past the function of God's community to get our hands on its forms. We've imagined that true Christian community results when churches are organized according to the biblical pattern, when denominational ties are eschewed, when we have the correct name above the door, and when we properly understand the doctrine of congregational autonomy. We have reduced community to agreement on the "Terms of Incorporation," and made conformity of opinion synonymous with an experience of the community of faith.

Indeed, we've often done worse. Allegiance to the forms of community has excused us to undermine and overwhelm the function of it. We quickly sacrifice fellowship over matters of structure and community methodology. We countenance division in the name of methodological purity. We act in the most belligerent, headstrong, bitter, and unloving ways to protect our organizational systems or the name by which we are called. We readily throw over every New Testament function of community in order to preserve any New Testament form of it.

Surely there is something wrong with that. Faithfulness demands that we build the same intimate community the early church was attempting to build; and get serious about loving each other as Christ has loved us; and develop a relational ethic rooted in the character of Jesus; and live as if we actually believe God will be glorified and the world convicted when Christians truly love each other.

Such a commitment will force us to adopt forms of community more radical than pot-luck dinners and compulsory attendance at baby showers. It may require us to abandon Sunday night gatherings in favor of small groups meeting in homes. It will encourage us to explore new forums for getting people together and encouraging dialogue that goes deeper than "Fine."[8] It will cause us to take seriously our responsibilities to accept, forgive and defer to each other. It will demand that we resolve conflict and rebuild broken relationships in the church.

It is the restoration of community function, not the reproduction of community forms, that is the true goal of people who want to build a biblical church. If fresh forms will encourage our people to know one another better and share with each other more deeply, we should explore those new forms so that we can be faithful to old functions. Clinging to old forms that have ceased calling us to an intimate experience of family is not "faithfulness." Indeed, devotion to ineffectual forms represents a greater threat to the church than small groups and donuts ever could.

God's People are Called to Mature Each Other

It was he who gave some to be apostles, some to be prophets, some to be evangelists, and some to be pastors and teachers, to prepare God's people for works of service, so that the body of Christ may be built up until we all reach unity in the faith and in the knowledge of the Son of God and become mature. (Eph. 4:11-13)

It is striking how *deliberately* the first-century church called its members to maturity. Baby Christians were rooted in the "knowledge of Christ" and in the Scriptures and in the teachings of the Apostles.[9] They were expected eventually to move beyond milk to the meat of God's word (1 Cor. 3:1-2; Heb. 5:11-14). Every document in what eventually became the New Testament was written as a "training" document—intended to educate and develop less mature Christians.

The specific task of church leaders was to help God's people become "mature, attaining to the whole measure of the fullness of Christ" (Eph. 4:11-16; Titus 2:1-15). Appropriate Christian living was consciously modeled by mature members of local congregations—and fledgling Christians were admonished to watch and imitate.[10] Those who were older in the faith were expected to actively train those who were younger. Mentoring relationships were purposely established—an apostle or evangelist or elder or older woman would "adopt" some younger Christian with the intention of growing the next generation of church leadership.

Through word and example, by careful study of Scriptures, by means of wise advice about practical living, and through veteran/rookie relationships, the early church entrusted the faith, lifestyle, and mission of Christ to "reliable men who will also be qualified to teach others" (2 Tim. 2:2; 1 Thess. 2:6-12).

Why did they do this? They were simply participating in the kingdom business of the Godhead. They were imitating the work they saw their Father doing with Abraham and Moses and the nation of Israel. They were honoring the patient labor of Jesus as he worked with the Twelve. They were recognizing their partnership with the Spirit in helping people "grow up in Christ."

Seeing this emphasis so clearly in the ancient church, it is sad to observe how this entire portion of kingdom business has dropped through the cracks in so many churches today. Where maturity is concerned, it is not that we have confused form and function. Rather, we have largely abandoned both the function of maturing the next generation and the forms used by the New Testament church to accomplish that end.

That is not to say there isn't real spiritual growth taking place in members of our congregations. There certainly is. People are "growing up in Christ." But, often, it is happening *accidentally* rather than intentionally; in spite of our efforts, not because of them. Maturing takes place serendipitously, not as the result of deliberate and planned intervention on the church's part. We do maturity by osmosis. Put new Christians into the church for long enough and they will absorb much of the church's culture and lifestyle. Let them develop some Christian friendships and peer pressure alone will produce the maturity newer Christians need to experience.

All of which is good. It's just not good enough. Is there nothing more intentional we should be doing to help people mature as Christians? Just because we have a sermon every Sunday and Bible

classes and mid-week services does not necessarily mean we are training tomorrow's church how to be disciples. Disciple-making will not
happen automatically if only we ensure that church members "do
not forsake the assembly." Familiarity with and unquestioning
acceptance of the cardinal tenets of Restorationism does not a disciple make. More is required to mature young Christians than a
Timothy class and an occasional Coke with the youth minister.

Yet, when "more" is attempted, we get nervous. Even when
churches borrow New Testament forms to address this biblical
function, they run into significant opposition. We have been so
frightened by the "Discipling Movement" that it is difficult even to
use the word "discipleship" without being accused of "cultish"
tendencies. The suggestion that we consciously pursue a plan for
mentoring baby Christians is greeted with suspicion and defensive-
ness. Pointing out mature Christians in a congregation and encouraging others to follow their example is said to promote pride and a
"following after mere men." We have systematically shot down
many of the New Testament forms used for maturing members of
the church. We have neglected to develop other forms that would
address the same function. And thus we have largely excused ourselves from a task Jesus and his apostles took very seriously.

People who are serious about restoration will take seriously the
mandate to grow up the next generation of Christians. Having seen
this commitment being lived out in the life of the ancient church,
they will renew that commitment in the life of the contemporary
church. They will do so not because they are devoted to a strict imitation of New Testament churches but because they are devoted to
the essential work they see taking place in the heavenly realms.
They will be serious about maturing people because they care about
the people whom God has entrusted to them—and they care about
the church those people will lead in the future.

God's People are Called to Serve

New Testament Christians were a ministering people. Whether that ministry involved helping others financially, opening their homes for hospitality, showing mercy to the sick or orphaned, encouraging the despondent, clothing the naked, visiting the imprisoned, healing, or simply listening—the first Christians understood that "pure and faultless religion" included serving people in need (Jas. 1:27). They knew they were called to use whatever resources and talents God had given them in pouring themselves out for others.

Looking back, we could ask how the ancient church served. We could identify who was served and what services were offered and under what circumstances. We could explore details about their collections and cooperative efforts and congregational sponsorship.

But somehow such questions miss the point. For the point of Christian service is not "how" but "why."

[W]hoever wants to become great among you must be your servant, and whoever wants to be first must be slave of all. For even the Son of Man did not come to be served, but to serve, and to give his life as a ransom for many. (Mk. 10:43)

For our spiritual forebears, ministry was an opportunity to participate in the selfless, sacrificial spirit of their Lord and Master. It was a chance to address the same "kingdom business" as Jesus. It was a way for Christians—individually or in concert—to bless others as God had blessed them. When faced with others' needs, and presented with an opportunity to help, these first Christians gave generously of their time, energy, and money for the privilege of serving.[11]

Thankfully, I see a revival of the "servant mindset" in Churches of Christ throughout this country. Overwhelmed by the physical, familial, social, and emotional needs of our neighbors, we recognize it is the function of service that is most important—not the forms by which service is rendered. Providing counseling, promoting literacy, holding marriage seminars, building life skills, caring for lost people in all their many guises—we are awakening to the centrality (and joy) of Christian ministry. Whether it be churches that band together to address the needs of inner-city minorities (as in Dallas, Memphis, and Los Angeles)...or churches that build homes for orphans or clinics for unmarried mothers or half-way houses for substance abusers...or members of Churches of Christ who serve soup at a kitchen run by the Salvation Army or distribute clothing at the Methodist Mission downtown—we have abandoned much of our fastidiousness over the ways and means of ministry in favor of getting at the essential business of ministry itself.

Even here, of course, it has been a challenge to prevent the forms of service from taking precedence over the function. Debates about the "right way" to minister, rather than ministry itself, have consumed us in times past. While we searched for New Testament guidelines on *how* service could be rendered—under what conditions, the procedures to be followed, and the cooperative pitfalls to be avoided—we often missed the generous, sacrificial, joyful, Christ-like function that ministry filled for the first Christians.

That said, I rejoice over the increasing sensitivity to the priority of service among Churches of Christ. People who take on the mind of Christ long to pour themselves out for the good of others. Whether it be ministering to brothers and sisters or to some beaten-down stranger at the side of the road, we have heard an echo of Christ's challenge to become servants of all.

Let's just not confuse a commitment to service with a par-roting of first-century procedures. Precedents are fine, but ministry is better. Inferences are good, but selfless service is better. A first-century example may be instructive, but glorifying God by ministering to people takes priority over ancient methodology.

Day care centers and mothers-day-out programs might not have been used by the church in Corinth. But they serve legitimate needs in our world today. Literacy programs, life skills seminars, and marriage enrichment conferences would not have been forms of service available to Paul. But they provide legitimate outlets for ministry today. Offering counseling services or financial planning or crisis intervention to our communities may not conform precisely to established New Testament practices. But such things are certainly consistent with the first church's emphasis on the function of ministry.

It is the restoration of merciful function, not the reproduction of ministry forms, that must be the true goal of those who would build a biblical church. If fresh approaches will encourage our people to serve, if new methods will let us minister more effectively, then we must not fear adopting those new forms so that we can be faithful to ancient functions.

God's People are Called to Witness

Evangelism is surely the most recognizable of the church's seven functions. Most of us understand that the church is a "commissioned" people—charged with telling the good news of Jesus to a lost world. "I pray that you may be active in sharing your faith, so that you will have a full understanding of every good thing we have in Christ" (Phil. 6).

Why did the first Christians talk about Jesus? Why were they so eager to "gossip the gospel"? Why were they such effective evangelists?

In a word, they had witnessed and personally experienced the trouble to which their triune God would go in speaking good news. How important to the Father was preaching Gospel? He was willing to send his own Son. How much value did Jesus place on witnessing to a lost world? He would rather die than keep quiet. And what weight did the Spirit give to such matters? He was consumed with preparing, convicting, enlightening and, finally, transforming those sinners who heard the saving story.

These heavenly realities became very personal to the first Christians. They had experienced real forgiveness and transformation. They knew all about lost...and found. Grace was not a theological concept to them. It was a living reality in their lives. Talking about Jesus was a chance to testify to the power at work in their lives.[12] It was an opportunity to bear witness to the cross and resurrection.[13] It was an occasion to rejoice in good news and announce it to others. They loved to talk of a gracious God who went in search of lost people.

Jesus spilled out of these early Christians because Jesus had been poured into them so generously. They talked about Him to everyone. They would not shut-up!

Unfortunately, that is not our struggle—evangelistically speaking! Members of the Restoration Movement have—in these latter days—lost not only much of their passion for witness but their confidence that anyone "out there" is listening. Few of us would argue that we are *effectively* reaching the world with the gospel.

Part of this evangelistic impotence is due to the message we have chosen to emphasize. Rather than dwelling on the majestic story of God's saving work through Christ and the cross, we have stressed man's necessary response. Instead of telling the "good news," we have extolled the restored church.[14] Evangelism has been reduced, for many in our movement, to convincing rather than convicting. It involves changing minds rather than breaking hearts. We have offered the world proof texts instead of grace.

Partly, though, our evangelistic laryngitis is rooted in a confusion about evangelistic methods. We are content with forms inherited from a prior time and a different world. We are nostalgic for a time when people came to our buildings, heard a "gospel sermon," and responded to the invitation. Week-long (or, at least, weekend) gospel meetings remain an evangelistic form-of-choice in many places—in spite of the fact that we cannot persuade our own members to attend, much less run-away teens or divorcing couples.

And we are suspicious of efforts to "preach the gospel" using more contemporary tools. Television and video, computers and the Internet, concerts featuring Christian musicians or seminars addressing "felt needs," seeker services and dramatic presentations and Easter programs—all provide powerful ways of touching the people of our communities with the gospel message. Yet evangelistic innovators have suffered at the hands (or mouths) of people who can see no godly use for such modern tools.

Shouldn't we, as restoration people, be concerned to recover our evangelistic voice? Can't we be as bold, as innovative, as creative as Jesus was, as Paul was, in barging onto the world's stage and announcing good news?

Restoration people will place a high priority on telling the story of Jesus. But they will not confuse the call to witness with a stubborn commitment to forms that no longer work. If old forms remain effective in bringing people to faith, let's continue to use them. But ineffective forms must be discarded and new forms, with greater promise, must be explored. The commission to "Go and make disciples" takes priority over methods that, while comfortable to us and revered in our tradition, no longer work in the world in which we live.

God's People are Called to Influence their World

You are the salt of the earth. You are the light of the world. (Mt. 5:13-14)

Finally, New Testament Christians tried to make a difference in the moral, relational, and cultural atmospheres in which they lived. In divorce-rife cultures, Christians were told to stay married. With time, Christian couples changed husband/wife, male/female interaction at a societal level. Christian slave-owners modeled a different kind of relationship with their slaves than was the norm, sounding a distant death-knell for the institution of slavery. In these and other ways, their consistent morality eroded the unjust and unethical habits of their culture.

But Christian influence in the early centuries was not simply a by-product of individual Christian ethics. There was a deliberate, intentional attack on the kingdom of darkness by the kingdom of light. And in this, once again, the early Christians demonstrated their commitment to participating in the work of their world-changing God.

Favoritism, prejudice, class-distinctions, and immoral lifestyles were forbidden within churches and confronted in the surrounding cultures. Idolatry, public and private vices, and hurtful traditions were not just condemned but actively battled by church leaders. The concerted efforts of Christians to relieve victims of famine, poverty, violence, and disease shamed their contemporaries into more humane (or, better, "Christian") behavior. Christian standards and attitudes began to permeate pagan cultures and set the moral tone not only for the church but for society at large.

So, what is the "saline content" of today's church? This is another area where (as with disciple-making) the Restoration Movement has largely ignored both the function of "salting" our world and the forms used by the New Testament church to accomplish that end. There has been a strident "separatist" theme in much of our preaching and teaching. So fearful were we of the world's influence that we argued for an arms-length relationship—in which neither the world nor the church posed much of a danger to the other. To avoid the threat of contamination, we opted for the safety of quarantine.

Thus, restoration churches were largely silent on the issue of race and social justice, both in the mid-1800s (slavery and the Civil War) and the mid-1900s (prejudice and Civil Rights). When other churches raised concerns about poverty, illiteracy and crime, we heaped charges of preaching a "social gospel" and "being more concerned with stomachs than souls."[15] While privately applauding protests against abortion clinics and boycotts to curtail the spread of pornography, we refused to engage these issues in a public and corporate manner.

We have not seen such "worldly" issues as our concern. Our mandate involves personal salvation, not social change.

But that was not the view of the first-century church nor of our first-century Lord. They did not shrink from speaking to and impacting the critical social issues of their day. Shouldn't we, as restoration people, be as willing to engage and influence our culture?

God intends for us to have a greater involvement with the world in which we live than the occasional stern lecture and shaken finger. Too many of our churches live out their institutional lives oblivious to the very real hurts and needs of their communities. Isolated and insulated, we restrict Christian duty to the church building or to the church family, and ignore the imperative to make a difference in the world around us. Sadly, by taking the "social" out of "gospel," we have ignored our commission and reduced the church and its message to the peripheries of our culture.

Restoration people will take seriously the mandate to make a difference. They will attempt to be salt in their world. Seeing this commitment lived out in the lives of Jesus and his first followers, they will renew that commitment in the life of the contemporary church. They will *intentionally, deliberately* find ways to impact their communities in the name of Christ.

Conclusion

This chapter has been painful to write—and, no doubt, to read. It has traced each of the seven functions through the heavenly realms and the early church to the attitudes and actions of contemporary Churches of Christ. In each case, we have seen something troubling. Rather than imitating the early church's commitment to join their Master in the work of the kingdom, we have often chosen to focus on the means and methods they used in getting that business done. Proper form has become more sacred to us than effective function. If we are not careful, we open ourselves to the charge that we would prefer to abandon the business of the kingdom than risk doing it the wrong way.

But I hope you have also seen something hopeful in these pages. It is possible to be a "restoration people" and yet pursue a very different agenda. When priority is placed on the business God has given his church to accomplish, when what we attempt to restore are not ancient methods but "eternal theological principles," when our focus becomes what God calls his people to do rather than how the first-century church did it—we are freed to restore what is at the center of the church's faith and practice.

I want to belong to a church that focuses on its functions: passionate about worship and living holy lives, pursuing intimate relationships and growing people up in Christ, bold in its ministry and witness, committed to making a difference in the world. I want to be part of a church that defines "obedience" and "faithfulness" by *what* it does, not *how* it does it.

God is calling us to imitate Christ and the early church, to pattern ourselves after the model we find in them. But it is not a pattern built around first-century methods and forms. It is rather a pursuit of the same kingdom business to which they dedicated themselves. God is calling us—first and foremost—to *function* like our Master and our church forebears.

When we commit ourselves to restoring those purposes that shaped the work of Jesus and his disciples, God will grant us the same freedom he gave them—to adopt whatever forms are available and appropriate to effectively address godly functions. Rather than doing "Bible things in first-century ways," we are free to do Bible things in contemporary and effective ways. What's critical is that we do "Bible things"—and that our methods support rather than hinder the doing of them.

Will we make mistakes as we explore fresh methods for doing old business? Certainly. Will we wander down blind alleys and fruitless paths? No doubt. Will our failures number more than our successes? Probably.

God's people have never been immune to failure. Wrong turns and poor choices are the church's stock-in-trade. Fortunately, we serve a God who can handle our failures. What is more difficult for him to handle is a fear of failure that leads his church to bury its business in the ground.

Form ever follows function.

Louis Kahn

Section III/ The Problem with Forms

We live in a world bounded by laws. The law of gravity insists that all things fall toward the center of the earth. The second law of thermodynamics asserts that energy and matter move from order to chaos—that everything breaks down. Murphy's law predicts anything that *can* go wrong *will* go wrong.

These are inescapable realities we cannot ignore. They are "constants" we fit our lives around. We watch our step when climbing stairs in mute submission to the law of gravity. We repair and repaint and restore in sullen acknowledgement of the power of entropy. We plan for contingencies and build in redundancies even while hoping—this time—things will go right. It doesn't matter that such principles are inconvenient and discomfiting. It is not relevant that we might prefer things work differently. We still must take these laws into account and treat them with great seriousness. To ignore them would be foolish…or insane.

Just as we acknowledge such physical laws governing the way things work in this world, so also do we acknowledge spiritual laws governing the way things work at the juncture between the flesh and the spirit. The cycle of Judges is one such "constant" we recognize and fit our spiritual lives around. We are "caught" in a spiritual loop that runs from faith to forgetfulness to falling away to suffering and, finally, to forgiveness and faithfulness once more. This is not a convenient reality. We all wish our lives would work differently. But we cannot ignore it simply because the cycle says unflattering things about our fickleness and calls us to engage frequently in the difficult work of repentance.

There is a similar but less familiar law that speaks to some hard realities about another aspect of religious life. Religion (whether expressed by individuals, congregations or movements) moves inexorably from a focus on function to an obsession with form, from a sensitivity to the central to a preoccupation with the peripheral, from an appreciation of what matters to a passion for what doesn't. There is a commanding immodesty about religious forms that forces them to the center of our attentions, overwhelming our sense of the important and demanding far more of us than they deserve.

Like other "laws," this law of spiritual entropy is not convenient or comfortable. We wish things could work differently. But in the end we must take this reality into account and treat it with great seriousness. If we don't, if we ignore or actively deny that such a process is at work, we set the stage for a great deal of spiritual folly to play out.

Already we have noted this process at work in our restoration heritage. Now the time has come to explore the process more carefully, to see how and why it exerts such a powerful influence on people of faith. The three chapters in this section represent an attempt in this direction. Chapter Seven examines the process at work in the faith of Israel and speaks to the conflicted relationship between form and function we discover there. What begins in symbiosis, moves to competition, and ends with a fight to the death. Form supports function, then eclipses function, and finally prevents function.

Chapter Eight looks at this conflicted relationship as it plays out in the Pharisees. How could Pharisaism devolve from a revival movement to a sect squabbling over hand-washing and tithing seeds? They provide an excellent, if painful, example of a religious group who allowed the forms of religious observance to overwhelm godly function.

Finally, Chapter Nine suggests a paradigm for better understanding the interplay between form and function. There is a natural life span for religious forms. Once vibrant and helpful forms lose their vitality with time and, eventually, cease to serve. Holding on to dead forms is one of the greatest acts of unfaithfulness the church can commit. How strange, then, that so many of us see such stubbornness as the very essence of keeping faith.

What follows is not pretty. You may find it disturbing. I do. But we cannot afford to look away. This is a reality the people of God must acknowledge and address. If, that is, we are determined to keep form in its proper place—at function's feet.

He who lightly esteems hand-washing will perish from the earth.

The Talmud

7/ Form Against Function

The largest bell ever cast is the Emperor's Bell. Weighing 440,000 pounds and measuring almost 23 feet in diameter, this gargantuan was specially made to commemorate the coronation of Tsar Kolokol III. Unfortunately, it was so huge it proved impossible to hang. When workmen attempted to hoist the bell into position, it fell, breaking a twelve-ton "chip" off the lip.

The Emperor's Bell never rang. For a while, it was actually used as a small chapel. At present, it serves as a gigantic street decoration[1]—and as a great illustration of how form can so overwhelm function that function is lost entirely.

A bell can be beautiful or unique or titanic in proportions. But if it can't be sounded, what good is it? Bells are made for ringing. That is their function. When the bell's form overwhelms that function, it ceases (in some meaningful sense) to be a bell.

A Lamentable Pattern

Form is never neutral. It either serves function or gets in the way. It follows function or works against it. That's true for bells or buildings or government or technology. And it is also true for the church.

Religious forms will always serve or hinder religious functions. They either help the church accomplish its mission or get in the way and keep the church from doing what God has commanded.

Of course, we have already noted this truth. We've seen examples of it in the uneasy relationship our movement has with the forms we have adopted from the early church and from our restoration forebears. Some of those forms help us do kingdom business. Some of them hinder.

With this in mind, let's consider a lamentable pattern, repeated often in Scripture and in the experience of God's church:

form follows function ⟶

form eclipses function ⟶

form prevents function

If you compare the business of the kingdom to a waltz, the "dance" begins with function leading and form following. Function drives form. Form follows function. Gradually, however (and without interrupting the dance), form and function change roles. Form begins to assert itself until, in the end, it has not only usurped leadership but managed to step all over the toes of its partner.

The failure to recognize this tendency (and to address it frontally) has been a source of great trouble for our movement. We have often been oblivious to the shift between form-for-the-sake-of-function to form-for-the-sake-of-itself. We've held to certain forms long after they ceased to serve the functions for which they were designed, not realizing that the very act of preserving disconnected forms can keep the people of God from accomplishing their vital mission.

Too often among Churches of Christ form has stormed the castle and enthroned itself as king. Function has been relegated to a subservient role. And we have stood in the gallery to applaud.

But that does not make us unique. In fact, the history of God's interaction with humanity underscores this same pattern and predilection. Take the nation of Israel, as an example. Judaism was

God's attempt to create a people who would *function* in a manner pleasing to him. What God envisioned with the calling of Abraham and Moses and David was an Israel existing as a holy, worshipful, compassionate, spiritual community—a religious Eden in a spiritually barren world. He wanted a relationship in which he would be Israel's God and they would be his people. The *forms* God gave to Israel (that panoply of ceremonial, moral, and social laws delivered through Moses) were intended to underscore function, to remind Israelites of and focus them on what God had called them to be. The forms themselves were never the point. They always harked back to something more fundamental and essential than themselves.

Yet even these God-given forms—clearly specified and carefully explained—had certain problems. Some forms, like the year of Jubilee, were apparently still-born—they never enjoyed widespread acceptance and use.[2] Other forms, like the site of worship (altar, tabernacle, or temple?) or the mode of governance (patriarch, judge, priest, or king?), were forced to evolve according to the changing conditions in which Israel found herself. (I'll say more about this in Chapter Ten.)

And a few forms suffered that inevitable devolution in which once living forms become dead ritual and eventually overwhelm the purposes they were originally designed to support.

That the three most prominent examples of this lamentable pattern in the Old Testament can be drawn from the three most central practices of Judaism is not without irony. When Moses came down from Sinai bringing commandments about circumcision, sacrifice and the Sabbath, he was instituting religious forms that were directly connected to religious functions. In each case, these *means* of expressing religious devotion were closely tied to the *ends* God was promoting among his chosen people. The functions were primary. The forms were secondary and supportive. Form followed function.

With time and habituation, however, each of these forms eclipsed the very functions they were intended to serve. Israel began to focus on the more tangible forms while neglecting the intangible but essential functions. Observing these religious forms *became* the function, as, slowly, the Israelites forgot what God was attempting to make of them.

Eventually, as we will see, form actually prevented function. Forms divorced from functions dominated the religious practice of Israel during the days of the prophets and Jesus. By clinging obstinately to dead forms, people like the Pharisees subverted the very functions those forms were instituted to support.

Circumcision

It would be difficult to find a religious form more central to Judaism than circumcision. On the eighth day after birth, every Jewish male was circumcised by the local rabbi. "The Circumcision" was another way of saying "the Jews." It became the mark, *par excellence*, to distinguish Jew from Gentile.

Yet circumcision was less about foreskins than about covenant. It was instituted by God as a *sign* of the covenant he had made with Abraham. "You are to undergo circumcision, and it will be the *sign of the covenant* between me and you" (Gen. 17:11).

Reconfirmed by Moses at Sinai, this mark on all Jewish males was intended as an ever-present reminder that promises had been exchanged, vows and responsibilities undertaken, between Yahweh and Israel. If circumcision was the form by which that covenant was commemorated, it was the covenant itself that was the function.[3]

With the passing of the years, and with the gradual habituation of the Israelites to the rite of circumcision, cutting off the foreskin ceased to *symbolize* covenant and became *synonymous* with it. Circumcision "of the flesh" (being so much more tangible than that "of the heart") became the principle means of identifying who belonged to God. A "child of Abraham" was increasingly defined as a "circumcised descendant of Abraham"; not someone who, like Abraham, had exchanged promises with God and lived in obedient relationship with him. An Israelite was someone who had been outwardly circumcised—whether there was any internal submission to Israel's God or not.

Jeremiah railed against his countrymen for this kind of thinking. Apparently, some of his contemporaries believed that a foreskin bought God's favor—even if a commitment of the heart did not accompany the surgery.

> "Circumcise yourselves to the LORD, circumcise your hearts, you men of Judah and people of Jerusalem, or my wrath will break out and burn like fire because of the evil you have done—burn with no one to quench it…The days are coming," declares the LORD, "when I will punish all who are circumcised only in the flesh…." (Jer 4:4; 9:25)

Evidently, these people had confused physical circumcision with obedience to God. Circumcision no longer *signified* covenant for them. It had become an end in itself, securing the promises of Yahweh without binding the people in any deeper way to their God. Jeremiah's harsh words attempted to remind the Israelites that there was more to being a Jew than going under the knife. *Heart circumcision* is the prime factor in determining who is pleasing to God.

Paul would later argue the same point:

> The one who is not circumcised physically and yet obeys the law will condemn you who, even though you have the written code and circumcision, are a lawbreaker. A man is not a Jew if he is only one outwardly, nor is circumcision merely outward and physical. No, a man is a Jew if he is one inwardly; and circumcision is circumcision of the heart, by the Spirit, not by the written code. (Rom 2:27-29)

"Circumcision is not covenant," Paul insists. Relationship to God involves more than submitting to circumcision. In fact, relationship is possible *without* circumcision (as Abraham and his spiritual descendents—Gentile Christians—prove). What Paul will not allow is making circumcision synonymous with covenant. Contrary to the thinking of some, an outward and physical circumcision does not make someone a Jew. Keeping covenant is the essence of faith, whether circumcision is present or not.

So circumcision, which began by pointing to covenant, gradually upstaged covenant and commanded more attention than was its due. But that is not the end of the story. Eventually, circumcision *prevented* covenant—the very thing it had been invented to serve!

We see it first in the reluctance of the Jerusalem Christians to preach about the New Covenant beyond the borders of the circumcised. The working assumption of the Jewish church was: "If they're not already circumcised, we're not going to tell them about Jesus." Circumcision (or the lack of it) initially prevented Jews from sharing the gospel with Gentiles.

We see it next in the insistence of Jewish Christians that Gentile believers be circumcised. "Unless you are circumcised, according to the custom taught by Moses, you cannot be saved" (Acts 15:5). Circumcision was trotted out as a *condition* of covenant relationship with God. Rather than let go of their cherished form, some Jewish Christians were willing to deny relationship with God to anyone who would not submit to it. They would condemn people who, through faith, had been "circumcised in the putting off of the sinful nature, not with a circumcision done by the hands of men but with the circumcision done by Christ" (Col. 2:11).[4]

Finally, we see how circumcision prevented covenant when it was used as an issue to divide churches, confuse Gentile believers, cudgel Paul, and undermine the effectiveness of his ministry. In defense of circumcision, Judaizers were quite willing to stir up trouble in newly founded and vulnerable communities of faith. They did not hesitate to muddy the waters for Gentile converts, "bewitching, " "enslaving," and "alienating" baby Christians (to use a few of Paul's words describing their work to the Galatians).

For the sake of circumcision, they maligned and attacked Paul's character and apostleship and gospel. They would have shut Paul up entirely, emasculating his ministry in order to protect their precious rite.

So here is the terrible pattern, illustrated by circumcision:

circumcision initially signified relationship ➞
circumcision became synonymous with relationship ➞
circumcision eventually prevented relationship.

Sacrifice

Sacrifice was another form central to the practice of Judaism. On holy days, under certain circumstances, as a means of expressing repentance or gratitude, Jews offered up to God the prescribed animals in the prescribed place according the prescribed rites.

But don't mistake the offering for the point. Sacrifice was a religious form used by God to highlight an essential religious function—*holiness*. God was never interested in creating a people who knew how to kill lambs correctly. He wanted a people who understood the importance of righteousness and the terrible cost of sin. God's intent was that Israel should be a holy nation, valuing the right and the good.

Because Israel found it difficult to achieve holiness, some allowance had to be made for sin. The sacrificial system codified by Moses was a form intended to remind Israel that sin costs, that it is a matter of life and death, that a holy God requires blood when dealing with an unholy people. When an Israelite placed his hands on a lamb (symbolically transferring his sins to the condemned animal) and then drew a knife across its throat, he was reminded in the most graphic terms that Yahweh takes holiness seriously and expects his people to do the same.[5] So long as the sacrificial system remained a vivid means of encouraging Israel to live pure and God-like lives, the sacrificial form continued to serve the holiness function.

Again though, as with circumcision, what started out in a subservient role quickly usurped the place of the very function it was intended to serve. Notice the chilling progression.

sacrifice initially signified a commitment to holiness ➞
sacrifice became synonymous with holiness ➞
sacrifice eventually prevented holiness.

Over time, as Israel grew accustomed to and even casual about the altar and the sacrifices, she came to regard sacrifice as synonymous with holy living. Get the sacrifices right, offer the right animal in the right way, go through the proper motions at the altar, and you have done what God required. Gradually, the faith of Israel shifted from a call to righteousness supported by the sacrifices to a religion of sacrificial appeasement that made few demands on personal righteousness. So long as the altar stood in Jerusalem and a priesthood existed to consecrate the required offering, the people of Israel could go on with their lives as though God had never called them to "be holy as I am holy."[6]

With the marriage of sacrifice and holiness (in which the two became one and the same thing), it was only a short step to their complete divorce. Wicked kings could make sacrifices to God and see no essential contradiction between their ritual and their lifestyle. Priests (like the sons of Eli) could defy God with their behavior and still conduct their altar duties with a straight face. The people could come to the temple with their lambs and leave with clear consciences to live foul lives. The presence of the sacrifices provided an excuse for Israel to sin and undermined the message of holiness they were originally intended to convey.

It was the prophets who stepped forward to identify this perversion of the sacrifices and to call Israel back to the primary function for which the sacrifices were instituted. Listen to Jeremiah ask the important question:

> Will you steal and murder, commit adultery and perjury,
> burn incense to Baal and follow other gods you have not
> known, and then come and stand before me in this house,
> which bears my Name, and say, "We are safe"—safe to do all
> these detestable things? (Jer 7:9-10)

Hear Hosea condemn Israel's separation of sacrifice and personal holiness. Listen as he castigates Israel and her priests for seeking God with "flocks and herds" but not their hearts:

> The more the priests increased, the more they sinned
> against me; they exchanged their Glory for something disgraceful. They feed on the sins of my people and relish their
> wickedness....
> Israel's arrogance testifies against them; the Israelites,
> even Ephraim, stumble in their sin; Judah also stumbles
> with them. When they go with their flocks and herds to
> seek the LORD, they will not find him; he has withdrawn
> himself from them....
> For I desire mercy, not sacrifice, and acknowledgment
> of God rather than burnt offerings. (Hos. 4:7-8; 5:5-6; 6:6)

And hear Isaiah turn 800 years of religious tradition upside down as he derides sacrifice without holiness and portrays a God who prefers righteous people over merely religious ones:

> The multitude of your sacrifices—what are they to
> me?... I have more than enough of burnt offerings, of rams
> and the fat of fattened animals; I have no pleasure in the
> blood of bulls and lambs and goats. When you come to
> appear before me, who has asked this of you, this trampling
> of my courts? Stop bringing meaningless offerings! Your
> incense is detestable to me. New Moons, Sabbaths and convocations—I cannot bear your evil assemblies. Your New

Moon festivals and your appointed feasts my soul hates.
They have become a burden to me; I am weary of bearing
them. When you spread out your hands in prayer, I will
hide my eyes from you; even if you offer many prayers, I will
not listen. Your hands are full of blood; wash and make
yourselves clean. Take your evil deeds out of my sight! Stop
doing wrong, learn to do right! Seek justice, encourage the
oppressed. Defend the cause of the fatherless, plead the case
of the widow. (Isa 1:11-17)

The prophets understood, if no one else did, that sacrifice in the
absence of personal righteousness makes a mockery of religion.
What was important to God was the holiness function, not the sacrificial form. When sacrifice actually discouraged righteousness, it
was time to kill the form in order to resurrect the function.

Sabbath

Sabbath observance was the third person in the Jewish Trinity.
Along with circumcision and sacrifice, Sabbath formed the essential
center of Jewish identity and practice.

But like the other two, Sabbath was a religious form intended to
point beyond itself to something deeper.

> The Israelites are to observe the Sabbath, celebrating it
> for the generations to come as a lasting covenant. It will be
> a sign between me and the Israelites forever, for in six days
> the LORD made the heavens and the earth, and on the sev-
> enth day he abstained from work and rested. (Ex. 31:16-17)
> There are six days when you may work, but the seventh
> day is a Sabbath of rest, a day of sacred assembly. (Lev. 23:3)

At the heart of Sabbath observance was the notion of *submission*.
Yahweh reigned as Lord of Israel, and one of the ways the people of
Israel demonstrated that truth was by dedicating the seventh day to

rest and worship. Whereas circumcision signified inclusion in the covenant and sacrifice signified God's call to holiness, Sabbath signified Israel's willingness to let God be God. Isaiah captures this notion well:

> If you keep your feet from breaking the Sabbath and from doing as you please on my holy day, if you call the Sabbath a delight and the LORD's holy day honorable, and if you honor it by not going your own way and not doing as you please or speaking idle words, then you will find your joy in the LORD.... (Isa 58:13-14)

Certainly, Sabbath was about rest and worship. But, more to the point, Sabbath was about doing as God pleased (as opposed to "doing as you please") and following God's direction (rather than "going your own way"). It was about Israel submitting herself to the will of God in a tangible and regular manner—one day of rest signifying a yielded life.[7]

It did not take long, however, for Israel to forget the point of the Sabbath and to substitute an obsession with Sabbath regulations for submission. Religious scholars of the day debated arcane and detailed questions of Sabbath observance. Could a man wear a wooden leg on the Sabbath? Could he put in false teeth? Was it lawful to eat an egg laid on the Sabbath? "Some knots and not others could be tied or untied on the sabbath. Vinegar, if swallowed, could be used to relieve a sore throat, but it could not be gargled. No woman was to look in a mirror on the sabbath lest, seeing a gray hair, she might be tempted to pull it out."[8]

Meanwhile, the common Israelite felt increasingly free to ignore submission to God in other areas of life so long as his Sabbath observance was meticulous:

> Hear this, you who trample the needy and do away with the poor of the land, saying, "When will the New Moon be over that we may sell grain, and the Sabbath be ended that we

may market wheat?"—skimping the measure, boosting the
price and cheating with dishonest scales, buying the poor
with silver and the needy for a pair of sandals, selling even
the sweepings with the wheat. (Amos 8:4-6)

In this passage, Amos describes a person who would not think of
breaking the Sabbath but has no qualms about mistreating the poor
or cheating customers. Instead of the Sabbath being for him a symbol of wider submission to God, it had become an end in itself. Keep
the Sabbath and you *were* in submission—whether or not that was
demonstrated in any other part of your life.

In the end, meticulous observance of the Sabbath actually
worked to *prevent* submission to God's will. By the time of Jesus, the
Pharisees would forbid healings, condemn innocent people, and
plot to kill Jesus—all in the name of Sabbath observance. Once
again, we see the destructive pattern at work:

Sabbath observance initially signified submission ⟶
 Sabbath observance became synonymous with submission ⟶
  Sabbath observance eventually prevented submission.

Form Against Function

It seems so "right" to rush to the defense of religious forms, clinging to the practices of our forefathers, and claiming "faithfulness"
in so doing. Certainly the Pharisees thought so. But in fact such a
practice is dangerous. Dangerous not because there is something
intrinsically wrong with any particular form, but because there is
something wrong with the way we relate to *all* religious forms.

There is an essential immodesty to religious forms that makes
them unhappy with supporting roles. Sooner or later, they always
insist on being the star, hogging the lime light while forcing function into the shadows. The victories of circumcision over covenant,
sacrifice over holiness, and Sabbath over submission are just a few
examples of forms' insatiable appetite for center stage.

But that is unfair to forms. Because the real problem lies with those who use them. Ultimately, *we* are the star-makers, shoving form to the fore and elbowing function off stage. Cursed with that "vigilant religious instinct of man for the place where grace is to be obtained at the cheapest price,"[9] we understand that it is easier to practice a religion in which forms steal the show. We prefer to focus on ritual and rite than on righteousness and authentic relationship with God. It is more comfortable to sacrifice than be broken and penitent, to circumcise than keep covenant, to rest on the Sabbath than submit the whole life to God.

We elevate forms beyond their place because, in the end, we (like the Israelites) find it simpler to pursue a religion of forms than to take God seriously.

And that is the first reality we must grasp in thinking about the relationship between form and function. We can embrace and defend and maintain religious forms and convince ourselves that, in doing so, we are being faithful. But that is naïve and unthinking.

The truth is that there is always a tension between the practices we use and the purposes they serve. In the following chapters, we will explore other aspects of this tension. For now, it is sufficient to point out that something in us prefers form. Something in us favors form. We are drawn to form—to the point that, left to our own devices, we will promote form over function.

But what good is circumcision without consecration, sacrifice apart from holiness, or Sabbath divorced from submission? What use are "correct" religious forms when disconnected from the functions they were intended to support?

When faith's forms overwhelm its functions, faith ceases (in some meaningful sense) to be faith. At such times, faithful people take action. Better to break the mold and start over. Better to let go of the practice and get back to the purpose it was designed to sustain. Better to recognize that, at some point, forms can cease to help and become an impediment to God's will and God's work.

And for to make a bird or fowl of wood and metal to fly, it is to be done so as to beat the air with wings as other birds or fowls do; being a reasonable lightness, it may fly.

William Bourne, 1800s

8/ The Tyranny of the Tiny

Edward Rutherford, in his book *Russka*, tells an interesting story about the Russian Orthodox Church in the seventeenth century.[1] Isolated by distance and culture from the mainstream of Orthodox faith, certain churches began practicing behaviors that ran contrary to the wisdom of the Orthodox leadership.

At certain points in their service, these churches sang two Hallelujahs instead of three; they used a different number of communion loaves; they made too many genuflections.

But particularly troublesome was the manner in which they made the sign of the cross. The accepted way to cross yourself in the Orthodox Church was to place the thumb against the ring finger and raise the remaining three fingers. Non-conforming churches, in contrast, placed the thumb against the ring *and* little finger, raising only two fingers toward heaven. This became known as the infamous "two-fingered" sign—the practice these dissenters believed to be the pure and ancient custom.

By the seventeenth century, reforms were begun to bring such churches more into line with the rest of the Orthodox fold. In 1666, the Patriarch Nikon called a Great Church Council which agreed that raising three fingers rather than two was the proper way to make the sign of the cross. Those who continued their opposition to this practice were to be excommunicated as heretics.

The *Raskolniki* or *Schismatics* would have none of that. Shocked by the ruling, they saw such reforms as the work of the Antichrist and prepared themselves for the end of the world. They refused to pray for the Tsar, they stopped sending contributions to the church coffers, and they kept right on with their heretical practices.

In 1684, the Regent Sophia outlawed the Schismatics, ruling that they could be arrested and tortured, and decreeing that anyone who gave them shelter would lose all property. Dissident priests were butchered. Entire communities were wiped out. Eventually, many Schismatic congregations decided to take their own lives rather than yield to the will of church authorities. It is estimated that tens of thousands of Schismatics burned themselves in their church buildings. These ritual self-immolations continued sporadically until as recently as 1860.

It would be easy to dismiss the people on both sides of this struggle as confused and tragically off-centered. Who cares whether the sign of the cross is made by raising two fingers or three? Is God really concerned about the number of hallelujahs or how many times you bow down in worship? On the "religious priorities" continuum, such issues fall off the "trivial" end.

But to the Schismatics (and their opponents), these matters were of critical importance. These people were concerned with what it meant to be "faithful." Beneath all the bickering about numbers of Hallelujahs and raised fingers lay the more important issue of what "faithfulness" demanded of the people of God. Though we may argue with their conclusions, it's hard to argue with their zeal.

We can question, however, whether their zeal was "based on knowledge" (Rom. 10:2). Were these people contending for matters that mattered or had they become tyrannized by tiny things? Was their dissent a sign of faithfulness or spiritual folly?

The stories of religious people consumed with tiny matters could be multiplied.

For centuries, the Catholic church insisted that Mass be conducted in Latin—even when that language was long dead and neither the priests nor the communicants had any idea what was being said. Had you asked them why this stubborness about language, they would have answered "Faithfulness."

Quakers are remembered, in part, for their continued use of "thee" and "thou" hundreds of years after King James and Elizabethan English had passed from the vernacular. Had you pressed them hard enough about such anachronisms, they would eventually have raised the issue of "Faithfulness."

The Amish still cling to nineteenth-century practices in the face of twenty-first-century realities—eschewing electricity and internal combustion engines while proudly driving their black, horse-drawn carriages down the highways of Kansas and Pennsylvania. Stop one of them and ask "Why?" and he will insist the reason revolves around "Faithfulness."

We look at such practices and marvel. We confess ourselves to be amazed and amused by behaviors like these. We say that we cannot comprehend how anyone could cling to such outmoded customs in the face of a changing world.

But why are we so surprised? We've seen it all before. In the pages of the New Testament, we meet a group of people who, for the sake of "Faithfulness," majored in minor things and missed completely the most profound religious event in history.

Addicted to Little Things

As drawn by the Gospel writers (and, again I acknowledge that they painted this group with a broad and exceedingly negative brush), the Pharisees are stunning examples of the tendency of religious people to forget what is essential to religion in favor of what is superfluous. They are a case study in the promotion of the tiny over the central.

In the Gospel of Matthew, for instance, we are presented with a series of conflicts between Jesus and the Pharisees. (They clash over a dozen times in this Gospel alone. As we review a sampling of these, please read the texts that are indicated below.) Almost every one of these contests revolves around the question of what is religiously central, what is religiously peripheral, and how to behave when the two are in conflict.

Consistently in these verbal skirmishes, the Pharisees come to the defense of religious forms. Consistently, Jesus champions religious functions. They invariably choose form over function. He always chooses function over form. In the end, they killed him for refusing to be as enamoured as they were with tiny things.

Matthew's introduction to the Pharisees occurs when Jesus is not on the scene. Even in his absence, though, their instinct for the tiny comes through. In Matthew 3:7ff, the Pharisees arrive at the Jordan to hear the preaching of John. They do not, however, see themselves as subject to his message. Why not? Because John is preaching repentance whereas they stand confidently in the genetic shadow of Abraham.

> You brood of vipers! Who warned you to flee from the com-
> ing wrath? Produce fruit in keeping with repentance. And
> do not think you can say to yourselves, "We have Abraham
> as our father." I tell you that out of these stones God can
> raise up children for Abraham.

Why bother with penitence when you have pedigree? Why confess sin when you can claim to be kin? John insists that brokenness is required for entering the kingdom. But the Pharisees cling to the superficiality of ancestry. And the sides are drawn for the controversies that follow.

In their first clash with Jesus, the Pharisees are offended that he should eat with "tax collectors and sinners" (9:9-13). They are concerned about appearances and the risks of spiritual defilement that might come from such close contact. Jesus is concerned about something else. "It is not the healthy who need a doctor, but the sick. But go and learn what this means: 'I desire mercy, not sacrifice.'" These sinners are "sick" people; Jesus has come to make them well. Such people are at the very heart of his mission. For Jesus, it is worth breaking traditions and social boundaries and the accepted etiquette to function as physician and forgiver. In his mind, function takes precedence over form. But not in theirs. They prefer to keep their social forms, protect their reputation for piety, and sacrifice people they should be concerned to save.

Their second skirmish involves Sabbath behavior (12:1-14). The hungry disciples pick grain and eat it. A man with a withered hand has the temerity to seek healing. The Pharisees work themselves into a righteous lather about these incidents, both of which offend their concepts of proper comportment on the Sabbath Day. "'Look! Your disciples are doing what is unlawful on the Sabbath…' Looking for a reason to accuse Jesus, they asked him, 'Is it lawful to heal on the Sabbath?'" In both cases, Jesus colors outside the lines of their tightly regulated religious forms. And, frankly, he doesn't care. He insists that the mercy function is more important than compliance with Sabbath regulations. He teaches that even the Father permits his Law to be bent to accommodate higher functions.

> Haven't you read what David did when he and his companions were hungry? He entered the house of God, and he and his companions ate the consecrated bread—which was not lawful for them to do, but only for the priests. Or haven't you read in the Law that on the Sabbath the priests in the temple desecrate the day and yet are innocent?

But the Pharisees can't hear him. They have ears only for religious whispers, not for the booming thunder of great religious principles. They miss the message "So it is lawful to do good on the Sabbath," and miss the majesty of the healing Christ performs, so consumed are they with protecting their Sabbath customs.

Oddly, the very customs that encourage them to condemn Jesus for doing good on the day of rest do not discourage them from scheming on that same day to take Jesus' life. "But the Pharisees went out and plotted how they might kill Jesus." To their God-deaf thinking, healing is damnable when it transgresses their forms. Murder is justified when it protects their forms. And the tiny becomes the standard by which all else is measured.

In yet another instance, Jesus and the Pharisees battle over the meaning of purity (15:1-20). "Why do your disciples break the tradition of the elders? They don't wash their hands before they eat!" By this time, Jesus is at his limit with them. He knows they are offended by his lack of fastidiousness. He knows that, in their thinking, unwashed hands are the slippery slope to an impure heart. But he is fed up with their obsession with the tiny and their oblivion to the important. He accuses them of giving God their lips but not their hearts. He calls them "blind guides" and tells his disciples to leave them alone. And he condemns their focus on hands rather than thoughts and motives as the source of spiritual impurity.

> Out of the heart come evil thoughts, murder, adultery, sexual immorality, theft, false testimony, slander. These are what make a man 'unclean'; but eating with unwashed hands does not make him 'unclean. (Matthew 15:19-20a)

When Counting Goes to Seed

It is only when you turn to the twenty-third chapter of Matthew, however, that you begin to understand just how consumed the Pharisees are with religious forms, how intolerant Jesus is of their promotion of form over function, and how great a gap separates his understanding of religion from theirs.

The Pharisees are obsessed with hems and phylacteries, seating order at the synagogue, and proper religious titles. These matters have become for them the essence of religious practice. But what of sincerity? "They do not practice what they preach." What of worship? "Everything they do is done for men to see." What of humility? "They love the place of honor." In every instance, they have missed the heart of true religion in their pursuit of the trivial.

They make religion, says Jesus, a matter of externals—cleaning the outside of the cup and whitewashing the exterior of the tomb—while ignoring the internal greed and self-indulgence and hypocrisy and uncleanness that are the proper concerns of religious faith. How they appear rather than who they are has consumed their attention and exhausted their energies.

So angry is Jesus at this betrayal of religious function, he cannot seem to find words strong enough to condemn the Pharisees. He keeps reaching for stronger language, more damning invective, as the chapter progresses. "Hypocrites… sons of hell…blind guides… fools…snakes…brood of vipers…murderers…How will you escape being condemned to hell?" Jesus is serious about this. He hates the brand of religion practiced by the Pharisees.

Verses 23-24 comprise the heart of this chapter. Here, Jesus does more than list another objection to what the Pharisees have done to faith. He explains what he finds so detestable.

> Woe to you, teachers of the law and Pharisees, you hypocrites! You give a tenth of your spices—mint, dill and cummin. But you have neglected the more important matters of the law—justice, mercy and faithfulness. You should have practiced the latter, without neglecting the former. You blind guides! You strain out a gnat but swallow a camel.

He tells them here the pith of their problem. Do you see it? They are counting seeds. They are ignoring what matters. They have a misplaced emphasis. And, consequently, they have become spiritually blind. Let's look at these four sad accusations, one painful point at a time.

1. They have focused on tiny things.

He begins with their fixation on tithing. Tithing, of course, was a religious form instituted by God, taught in the law of Moses, and required of all faithful Jews. The Pharisees were great tithers. They prided themselves ("I give a tenth of all I get"—Lk 18:12) on their diligence in this matter. But like all religious forms, tithing can be given more weight than it deserves. It is not, and never will be, an "important matter" in the economy of the kingdom.

But don't say that to a Pharisee. To them, tithing was a mark of "faithfulness" that distinguished the pious from the unwashed masses. They took it very seriously. According to Jesus, they were so meticulous about tithing that they counted seeds—"Nine for me, one for the Lord... nine for me, one for the Lord."

Perhaps this is another example of Jesus' hyperbole. Maybe they didn't really count seeds. But if Jesus exaggerates, he does so to make a point. He describes an orientation to religion in which forms like tithing have become the focus of religious life. For the Pharisee, honoring these forms defined and gave identity to "Faithfulness." By counting seeds, the Pharisees hoped to demonstrate their commitment to God.

2. They have ignored things that matter.

"But look at the opportunity costs," says Jesus. While the Pharisees are on their hands and knees sorting seeds into piles as proof of their piety, matters like justice, mercy and faithfulness go begging. They could be championing the cause of the poor and disadvantaged or feeding the hungry or building bridges to lost people. Instead, these deluded souls are tithing seeds and tying on phylacteries and measuring the distances they are permitted to travel on the Sabbath. Rather than choosing the "better part" and spending themselves on the "important matters," they neglected such things in their headlong pursuit of trivialities.

That's the sad flip-side of majoring in minors. You also minor in majors. Attention to one thing means neglect of the other. Jesus hammers on this point in what he tells them next.

3. They put their emPHAsis on the wrong sylLAble.

One of the hard realities about life in this world is that we are finite creatures, with limited time, energy, and attention. The decision to focus on one thing is—necessarily—a decision not to focus on another. The decision to spend an hour doing this means we cannot also spend the hour doing that. Energy devoted to one master means energy lost to another. It is an axiom of life.

The question always facing finite people, then, is "Where will you place your emphasis?" We cannot do it all. We are required to pick our battles and choose our focus. Similarly, the question facing finite *religious* people is, "What things must be emphasized in order to please God?" In other words, what defines 'faithfulness'?

The Pharisees knew how to answer that question. "We will get tithing right (and Sabbath and hand washing and oaths and food laws and dress codes, *ad infinitum*), and then work on justice, mercy, and the other stuff. We will be faithful in the tiny, and attend to the important as we have time and energy. First we get the forms of religion right and then we move on to the functions."

The problem is that the demands of the tiny are never ending. There is always one more detail to fix, one more ritual to attend to, one more issue to fine tune. Once you start giving emphasis to the tiny, there is no reasonable stopping place.

It isn't that the Pharisees were *against* justice and mercy and faithfulness. But who's got time left for such matters after a full day of inculcating hand-washing? Who has energy left after an exhausting session of Sabbath protection? Who can pay attention to big things when seed counting requires such vigilance and concentration?

They permitted tiny things to tyrannize them, to monopolize their time and energies, to consume their attentions. And, as a result, they had nothing left for the things that mattered.

Jesus answered the "emphasis" question very differently. "Emphasize the things that matter *first* and *then* devote whatever is left to the rest." He makes a clear distinction between the "more important" and the less important. He specifically recognizes that there are some things that are "weightier" than others. And he insists that the spiritually wise thing to do is to major in the major things and minor in those things which, in the final analysis, are minor.

It is a source of great amazement to me that these very words are so often put to use making *exactly the opposite point* Jesus is trying to make. "Practice the one without neglecting the other," some folks are quick to point out. What they mean to say is that Jesus does not give us permission to *ignore* less important things. Issues like tithing and Sabbath and circumcision do not go away simply because we give our first and best attentions to the weightier matters of God's law. Religious forms still demand some attention even when we decide to emphasize religious functions.

True enough. But read Christ's statement more carefully. Is he actually saying, "Practice the more important matters, but don't neglect to tithe mint, dill and cummin"? Is he saying that, after we've given our best efforts to the weightier matters of the kingdom, we still have a responsibility to count seeds?

The way some of us use this passage, you might be tempted to think so. We embrace that *"without neglecting"* as a blanket command under which we fit every jot, tittle, detail, quirk, preference, and gnat within reach. This verse becomes our proof text that counting seeds is really not so minor after all. We cannot afford to neglect such matters. Follow that reasoning far enough and soon we are right back to the tyranny of tiny things—the small and minor and peripheral once again crowding the important out of our attentions and out of our lives.

But isn't it possible Jesus is saying something else? Could he be saying, "Get the important stuff right and you will know what to do with the rest. Put your emphasis where it belongs and other things will take on a proper perspective. Once you focus on what matters, you have a standard by which everything else can be measured."

In fact, some things deserve to be neglected—they are too tiny and peripheral to be worthy of our attention. Counting seeds, no matter how convicted the Pharisees were to the contrary, has no place in the life of a godly person. I cannot imagine Jesus taking time to engage in such an activity and I will not waste one more moment on such nonsense than he would.

And some things, though perhaps not neglectable, deserve far less time and energy than we currently devote to them. But only a dedication to the things that really matter can teach us how to put everything else in its proper perspective and proper place.

4. They suffer from a peculiar blindness.

It is the last line in his statement that contains the strongest warning: "You blind guides! You strain out a gnat but swallow a camel." The word "blind" keeps cropping up in this chapter—Jesus' favorite pejorative for the Pharisees after "hypocrites."[2] He calls them "blind guides" (twice), "blind fools," "blind men," and then "blind Pharisees."

Throughout, he chastises them for a particular kind of blindness—a *spiritual microscopia* that permits them to see tiny things but miss completely the obvious and the huge. When they cannot see past the wording of an oath to the issue of character and integrity that is at stake, they are blind. When they can see only the external, but not the corruption that lies inside, they are blind. And when they can't tell the difference between things that matter and things that don't, they are blind.

Once again, Jesus borrows the language of hyperbole to illustrate the sort of blindness from which the Pharisees suffer. According to Jesus, people who spend more time counting seeds than showing mercy are also likely to be sharp-eyed for gnats but myopic about camels. They see (and strain out) the smallest speck, the tiniest mote. But they are quite oblivious to the camel sitting in their cup. So, carefully removing the one, they swallow down the other.

That's what the tyranny of the tiny does. It makes one blissfully ignorant of the important. It induces a focus on the trees rather than the forest. It measures life with a micrometer and only admits the reality of those things that fall somewhere between trivial and unimportant. The tyranny of the tiny doesn't induce total blindness—just blindness to things that matter.

But it does more. The tyranny of the tiny persuades you to believe that the tiny is actually the important, that the minor is major, that the unimportant is, in reality, the very thing around which the sun rises and sets. It is the tyranny of the tiny that makes you want to burn down a church building full of people who would dare to use the two-fingered sign in crossing themselves. It causes you to look with suspicion on those who worship in non-Latin, or use electricity, or utter modern pronouns. The tyranny of the tiny makes you want to kill when somebody heals on the Sabbath Day.

I called this problem *spiritual microscopia*—and that aptly describes the blindness of the Pharisees. When you look at life through a microscope you never see the mountains. What you do see are speck-sized issues magnified to mountainous proportions.

This is what Jesus hated about Pharisaism. This is what he found so pernicious about their practice of faith. In their worship of the tiny, they neglected what was important, they ignored what mattered, they had eyes only for gnat-sized truths. By deifying details, they turned the kingdom of God on its head, valuing what was worthless and disdaining what was vital. They called good evil and evil good.

He hated Pharisaism because, in defining religion by the tiny, they turned the kingdom into something that had no meaning to anyone outside their tight circle, that had no relevance to the "sinners" of the world, that struck everyone but themselves as trivial and obscure and peripheral.

And, most of all, he hated Pharisaism because it painted God as the author of such a small, misshapen, spiritually perverse faith. It put God on his hands and knees counting those seeds with the Pharisees. It claimed that God was more concerned about Sabbath rules than people's needs, about washed hands than pure hearts. It made God look like a Pharisee.

And What about Us?

In the last chapter, we noted the temptation to promote form over function. It is so much easier to relate to God through externals than with the heart.

But in this chapter, we are confronted with a second truth about form and function. Form, once promoted above its proper station in faith, is a harsh tyrant. It allows no other competitors for our affections. It blinds us to more important matters, and so consumes our time and attention that we have nothing left for other concerns. People who allow themselves to be trapped by the tiny have a hard time getting away. They have a hard time understanding they need to get away.

It is so easy to see this in the life of other religious movements. We can point the finger at those who have lost focus on what is central and become distracted by the tyranny of the tiny. We pity the Pharisees for their preoccupation with Sabbath laws and hand washing. We look at the Schismatics and the Amish and recognize that they missed the central somewhere along the line.

But it is much harder to see how we ourselves are susceptible to the same religious disease. It is monumentally difficult to confess that, too often, our definition of "Faithfulness" has devolved to an unyielding preservation of peripheral but oh-so-sacred cows. You and I are not above being captured by the miniscule and defending to the death things that, in the end, just don't matter.

Not above it? Let's be honest. We've often majored in it. We have made defense of the tiny our stock-in-trade. We have argued over gnats. We have made war over spiritual specks. We've drawn lines and split and alienated over religious minutia.

Would to God that we could claim to be the great defenders of the gospel of grace, the sufficiency of the cross, the hope of the resurrection, the power of prayer. Oh that we had built a reputation as the champions of justice and mercy in a fallen world. But these are not the great theological mountains we have chosen to defend.

Rather, we have entrenched ourselves in defense of mole-hills. Clerical titles. Worship styles. Organizational structures. Peculiar hermeneutical systems. Women's role. No choirs. No instruments. Ugly architecture. Anti-hand clapping or raising. Slippery slopes. Shape notes.

The list goes on. But no one is listening. We might as well be talking about two-fingered signs and horse-drawn carriages. If *we* cannot see it, the world around us does—we are trapped in the tyranny of tiny things.

Look at the front page of *The Tennessean* for Sunday, May 23, 1999. Above the fold, the headline reads, "Goodlettsville officer, woman die in rampage." The accompanying article tells of the shooting deaths of a policeman and a 20-year-old woman, both killed by the woman's abusive and frequently-arrested husband. For the past month, the front page had been filled with news of school shootings in Colorado and Georgia, the war in Kosovo and the plight of the refuges, Chinese espionage, sexual assaults, drug busts, and political scandal.

But this particular Sunday, the front page headline below the fold read, "Church of Christ congregation's use of music creates echoes of discord." The article told of a local congregation that used an instrumental music recording in its Easter Sunday service, and the firestorm of controversy it sparked. A church-related, K-12 school nearby decreed that none of its faculty or staff could attend that church and keep their jobs. The preacher, caught between his ministry and the fact that his wife worked at the offended school, resigned his position rather than prompt her dismissal.

The comments of the reporter were telling. "What sounds trivial to outsiders is a potential cataclysm in the Church of Christ fellowship...." He then went on to list some further flash points of controversy among us. "Some churches are 'one-cuppers' who insist on serving communion from a common cup, not individual vials. Some insist on wine; other go with grape juice. Some refuse to hold Sunday School classes or build gymnasiums on church property."

The comments of a knowledgeable "source" were even more telling. "That's a crisis facing Churches of Christ. The worry is if you let the bar down, you lose your identity....The question is: Which of these practices is essential to belief? If you've spent your whole life building an identity on certain practices and all of a sudden those things are unimportant, where is your life?"

It would be one thing if this front page article were an anomaly, if it represented something counter to our reputation, if such controversies were uncommon and uncharacteristic. But the article is convicting, and cutting, precisely because it exposes us for what we are—a movement that has lost its focus on the central and become enamoured with tiny things. The article, so public and glaring, does what it should do. It embarrasses us.

It is embarrassing that our "identity" should be tied to such issues. The cross, yes. The lifestyle of discipleship, certainly. The centrality of grace and the Spirit and the community of faith, by all means. But the use of an instrument? One cup or many? A gymnasium? What does it say about us that we have spent our collective life "building an identity" around such issues, that we could "lose" our identity by playing a piece of recorded music on a Sunday morning?

And it is embarrassing that we should be defined to the world by such matters, that people would read in the Sunday paper that things which are "trivial to outsiders" are cataclysmic to us. What does it say to those readers that our "orthodoxy" centers around such arcane minutiae and (as the article goes on to comment) that such "Church of Christ orthodoxy" is enforced by "peer pressure and the threat of social blackballing"?

But it is beyond embarrassing. It is *mortifying* that, nestled among the daily fare of killing and seduction and war and hatred and greed, is an article that has the people of God addressing none of those issues. We're too busy policing each other's worship styles to make news about the way we are changing the world for God. We make the front page for our fascination with the tiny rather than for our commitment to weightier matters like justice, mercy, and faithfulness.

Perhaps this doesn't embarrass you. But I think it should. It is symptomatic of a peculiar blindness that afflicts those who have taken their eyes off of the central. It puts us, sadly, in common company with the Pharisees of Jesus' day.

A Brief Exercise in Self-diagnosis

Perhaps it is appropriate to use the accusations Jesus hurled at the Pharisees as a measure to hold up against ourselves. What is good for the Pharisees is good for religious people of all ages, our movement included.

Have we also focused on tiny things? Have we ignored the things that matter? Is our emphasis off-center? Do we suffer from *spiritual microscopia*?

I would suggest that when issues such as instrumental music, hand-clapping, the building of family life centers, translations of the Bible, etc. take on an importance that cleaves between the faithful and the unfaithful—when such things become the Shibboleths we use to define ourselves and our identity—we must seriously consider the possibility that we have allowed the tiny to take on an unmerited importance.

And when, in our busyness to pursue the tiny, we have allowed evangelism and meaningful service and disciple making and the building of intimate community to become matters we never quite get around to, we must have the courage to question whether we are neglecting the more important matters of the kingdom.

[As with the Pharisees, it's not that we are against justice, mercy, and faithfulness. But who's got time left for such matters after a day spent writing an article on the slippery slope of raising hands in worship? Who has energy left after an exhausting defense of command, example, and necessary inference? Who can pay attention to the larger issues when policing the use of instruments requires such vigilance and concentration?]

When gnats and spiritual micrometers and theological specks define the standard through which everything must pass; when we cannot hear a Christ-honoring message because the congregation clapped during a song; when we cannot participate in an effective ministry of mercy because the church sponsoring it has female deacons; when we cannot read and teach from a book on holiness because the author worships with an instrument; when we break relationship with brothers and sisters because the leaders of their congregation decide to encourage small group gatherings on Sunday night, we must examine ourselves to see if we suffer from the same kind of blindness afflicting the Pharisees.

If we allow ourselves to be so tyrannized by the tiny that we practice what is peripheral while neglecting what is central, we run the risk of turning the kingdom of God on its head, valuing the superficial and disdaining the vital. We risk turning the kingdom into something that has no meaning to anyone outside our tight circle, that has no relevance to the "sinners" of the world, that strikes everyone but ourselves as an exercise in the trivial and obscure. And, most of all, we risk portraying God as a deity who cares deeply about such trivia. We put God in our pews with his arms crossed and his face scowling because someone sang during the Lord's Supper. We portray a God who is more concerned about worship etiquette than broken hearts, about congregational autonomy than effective outreach. We make God look like us.

A Concluding, Unscientific Postscript

"Where is our life?" asks the "source" interviewed in the above article. I will answer. It is in Jesus Christ. It is in the proclamation of the gospel of God's grace. It is in the commitment to holiness and mercy and service. It has nothing to do with the musical forms we use in worship or the structures through which we cooperate to do mission work.

"How then," someone will ask, "do we distinguish ourselves from other religious groups?" The question betrays the unbiblical and self-defeating notions underlying our notion of "identity." If a commitment to the essential religious functions to which God has called his people, if allowing matters like gospel and ministry and witness to define us, causes inter-denominational confusion, so be it. Perhaps therein lie the seeds of the "oneness" Jesus prayed for on the night he was betrayed.

But the related question is more to the point. If distinguishing ourselves from other religious groups demands the adoption of a trivial creed, if we are forced (for the sake of identity) to elevate minor matters to the status of salvation issues, the price is too high. Better to lose our separate identity if, in so doing, we can be freed from the tyranny of the tiny and return to the unrelenting pursuit of things that matter.

Every age knows the temptation to forget that the gospel is ever new. We try to contain the new wine of the gospel in old wineskins—outmoded traditions, obsolete philosophies, creaking institutions, old habits. But with time the old wineskins begin to bind the gospel. Then they must burst, and the power of the gospel pour forth once more.

Howard Snyder

9/ A Life Span for Forms

Metaphor is a game we play with language. It is an inventive and forceful means of comparing one thing to another. Good metaphor allows us to draw an equal sign between two objects, using something with which we are familiar to help us understand something that is more difficult to grasp. For example, when Jesus says that we are to be the "light of the world" (Mt. 5:14), he intends for us to understand something about who we are and how we are to function by comparing our effect on the world to a light shining in darkness. It is precisely because we understand how light functions in darkness that we can learn something from this metaphor about the meaning of discipleship.

G. B. Caird, in his book *The Language and Imagery of the Bible*, makes some interesting observations about metaphors that will help us as we think about form and function in the church. According to Caird, metaphors have a life-span.[1] In the case of Jesus' use of "light," that span is very long. It is easy to recognize that Jesus is speaking metaphorically here and it is relatively easy to understand the point he is trying to make. Because we still deal with light on a daily basis, Christ's words remain a living metaphor—even modern readers get the point.

Through continual usage, however, metaphors become *faded* or stock. We still recognize that a figure of speech is being used— that a comparison is being made—but the point of the comparison is blunted because the familiar element is no longer familiar. When David says, "The Lord is my shepherd" or Jesus speaks of the "kingdom of God," we understand that they are attempting to explain spiritual realities using down-to-earth elements. But to the degree that we are not familiar with sheep and shepherds or kings and their kingdoms, the power and vividness of the metaphor is lost. We can clarify Jesus' meaning by educating ourselves about shepherds and kingdoms. But just as a joke that has to be explained is not as funny, so a metaphor that must be explained is not nearly so compelling.

The final stage in the life span of a metaphor is the *dead metaphor*—when we are no longer conscious that a metaphor is being used at all. Many of the clichés of a language are made up of dead metaphors that have passed directly into the vernacular: the eye of a needle, the brow of a hill, the mouth of a river (to cite just a few metaphors built on comparisons to the body). For most of us, "beating a dead horse" simply means engaging in some useless activity. We no longer think of some poor man trying to rouse his expired beast at the side of the road, and then say to ourselves, "Ah, that's just like me!" To be "on the rocks" means only that someone or something is in a bad state. No image of a ship foundering on the shoals, being beaten to pieces by the waves, comes to mind. We speak of such things all the time with no consciousness that we are speaking in metaphor.

Metaphor can be one of the most powerful forms of human expression—surprising, convicting, enlightening. Jesus used it frequently. But in time, many metaphors cause as much confusion as enlightenment because we no longer clearly understand the point they make. Eventually, the wording of the metaphors is all that's left; there remains no understanding of the meaning that lies behind them.

I find all this particularly interesting because the notion of a life span for metaphors corresponds so well to a reality about the forms we use to express our Christian life.

There is no such thing as a "formless religion." The people of God will always find ways, means, methods, and modes for expressing their adoration of and obedience to God. However, religious forms, like metaphors, have a life span. Some are extremely long-lived. Others die a quick death. But all forms are susceptible to a natural entropy. With time and overuse, they can (and do) lose their power to express adequately the functions to which the people of God have been called.

Living Forms

For God's people, *living forms* are those modes of expression, those tools for giving voice to our life before God, that continue to provide an eloquent means of fulfilling the functions God expects of his church. Songs that touch and move us, sermonic styles that allow us to hear God's word afresh, outreach methods that effectively lead people to Christ, fellowship activities that foster the kind of intimate community that God wants and we need, ministries that connect with the world and make a difference in our sinful culture—living forms allow the church to be the church and to do the kingdom business with which we have been entrusted.

Living forms are *fresh*. We have not habituated to them to such a degree that we can go through the motions of the form with little thought or personal involvement. By definition, you don't take living forms for granted. There is something surprising, something compelling about them. This "freshness" is not always the same as "newness." Some very old songs retain their ability to move us. Hospitality may be as old as Abraham, but it continues to be a vibrant means of promoting intimacy and building community. Often, however, the adage holds true—familiarity does breed contempt. It is harder for overly familiar forms to preserve their freshness from generation to generation.

Living forms are *effective*. They actually produce the fruit they were intended to produce. If the purpose of the form is to educate God's people about the Bible, then real learning should take place. If the purpose is to promote fellowship or to bring lost people to Christ, those forms effectively encourage brotherly love and a saving commitment to Jesus. Living forms are validated by the fruit they bear. We can point to transformed lives as demonstrable proof of the manner in which these forms support the eternal functions of God's people.

Living forms are *culturally appropriate*.[2] They permit the people of God to express themselves in words and actions that are appropriate for the times in which they live. When the Romans greeted each other with a "holy kiss" or Corinthian women covered their heads during the assembly, they were utilizing customs that were common to the day. When the church of the last century gathered for "arbor meetings" or three-month-long "readings," they too were practicing forms that were tuned to the times. None of these practices, however, are suitable for present purposes because all of them are out of step with the culture in which we live. A commitment to living forms—forms that are fresh and effective—necessarily means that we adopt forms that are culturally relevant and abandon those that have ceased to be meaningful in a contemporary setting.

Finally, and most importantly, living forms are *directly connected to the functions* they serve. We recognize how they are related to purposes the church is intended to pursue and the important role they play in helping us achieve those purposes. There is a clear understanding of *why* we employ these forms—it is because we want to be holy or to make disciples or to be salt to the world. The focus with living forms, however, is very much on the functions they support rather than the forms themselves. They are *means* not *ends*. My father once defined modesty for me as "dress that does not call attention to itself or to you." There is a modesty to living forms that keeps function at center stage. They do not assert themselves in such a way that our attentions are focused on the form rather than the purpose for which it is employed.

Faded and Dead Forms

With time and through continual usage, however, all religious forms grow *faded* or *stock*. Songs that once moved us are sung from memory and with little emotion. A Sunday night gathering—once an occasion for fellowship and encouragement—becomes a distasteful obligation. A ministry begun with great enthusiasm continues only out of a sense of duty and will power. The Supper—first eaten with a full heart and undivided attention—is now eaten out of habit while we try to keep the kids quiet. Those "eloquent means of fulfilling the functions God expects of his church" cease to speak for us as powerfully as they once did.

Count on it. Once fresh forms grow stale—we habituate to them and begin to take them for granted. Once effective forms lose their potency—they no longer produce the fruit they were designed for. Once appropriate forms become quaint and anachronistic—they are no longer suitable for present purposes because they are out of step with the culture in which we live. And forms that once were direct expressions of the functions we value grow increasingly remote and isolated from the business God has given to us.

We remember what these fading forms are *supposed* to do for us (perhaps even recall what they once did), but find that they lack their old power, vividness, productivity, and relevance. There is a growing disconnection between *how* we do things and *why* we do them. The *point* becomes confused. By a conscious act of will, we can pump new life into faded forms and experience again some remnant of their former strength. But to the degree that these forms have become habitual, they fail to evoke in us the emotions or attitudes or actions they once aroused.

Allow this trend to continue long enough and we find ourselves holding to *dead forms*—expressions of religious life in which predictability is more important than freshness, correctness is valued more than effectiveness, and tradition overwhelms relevance. Dead forms become, themselves, the point of religious activity—a sort of religious cliché we use reflexively but with little passion or understanding. Here, there is no deeper meaning, no conscious function to which the form calls us. *Enacting the form becomes the function.*

If we gather in a building bearing a certain name, with people who observe five acts of worship, *that* is worship, whether there is any movement of the Spirit or experience of the presence of God. If we hold an annual gospel meeting, *we have been* evangelistic, whether or not anyone came and heard and found life. When we "forsake not the assembling" of ourselves together, *we are being* a community of believers, whether anything passing for intimacy actually transpires.

Dead forms are the cold ashes of something that once burned bright and hot. We can gather around them and convince ourselves there is yet some religious heat to be found there. We can content ourselves with the memory of the warmth we once derived from them. We can even chastise those who shiver around the dead cinders for complaining of a chill.

But the reality is that every form of religious expression has a life span—caught somewhere on a continuum between fresh and stale, effectual and impotent, meaningful and rote, inspiring and vapid.

An Example of the Life Span of Forms

The songs we sing in worship provide, perhaps, the easiest illustration of this tendency for forms to live, fade, and eventually die. The words to "Night with Ebon Pinion" have moved many a generation to tears—especially during those times when words like "ebon," "pinion," "vale," and "smitten" were in common usage and easily understood. This song, when first sung, was a living form calling worshippers to contemplate the agonies of the garden on the night Jesus was betrayed. For subsequent generations, however, the power of this song faded. We could turn to our dictionaries and read that ebon meant "black," pinion meant "wing," vale referred to a "valley," etc. By explaining what the song meant before singing it, we could breathe new life into this old song and experience again the oppressive presence of that black night "brooding o'er the vale." Many of us, however, failing to understand the picture being painted by the poet, find ourselves singing words that have lost their meaning and, hence, their power to move us to worship. To the teenager who sits in our assemblies, that song is a dead form—devoid of meaning, a relic from a past he does not understand or appreciate, and one more proof that religion has little relevance to the kind of world in which he must exist today.

Recognizing that this hymn has seen its better days is not an act of unfaithfulness. It is not a criticism of our fathers' faith or a repudiation of the manner in which they worshipped. It is simply a realistic assessment that, while some of us may still enjoy singing that song, it is at the end of its useful life. For many in our congregations, this hymn has ceased to be fresh, effective, relevant, and worshipful. We can continue to prop it up by defining its words and explaining its poetic imagery whenever we sing it. But eventually we ought to wonder whether a new song, using contemporary words, might call us more effectively to reflect on Gethsemane. Which, after all, is more important: singing that particular hymn or bringing to mind what Christ endured because of his love for us? As Caird states, "because we live in a linguistically mobile world, we need to keep running if we are to remain in the same place."[3]

The same can be said of the musical styles we use in our worship services. Gregorian chants, antiphonal singing, the harmonies of madrigals and metrical Psalms and Appalachian folk tunes, canticles, motets—all are forms that have been used to encourage the church to worship. But, though each form began as a fresh means of expressing devotion to God, all, through habituation and overuse, eventually lost their ability to effectively usher the church into God's throne room. Once living forms of musical expression, faded and eventually died.

We experience something similar today in regard to Stamps-Baxter style songs. The strict verse-chorus arrangement, the strong bass lead, the counter rhythms and repetitive melodies—these were appropriate and even helpful styles during an era when barber shop quartets and "My Gal Sal" were all the rage. But to suggest that other musical styles are more appropriate to the modern church is neither an act of disrespect or a display of musical snobbery. It is simply a recognition that "Let's Just Have a Little Talk with Jesus" has outlived its usefulness to the contemporary church and should be replaced with modern musical forms that more closely reflect the times in which we live.

I can even give you an example of a song that, in the course of my life time, has experienced the entire span of its useful life. I remember being at youth camp, gathered around the fire at night, singing "Blue Skies and Rainbows" with great emotion and volume. That song encouraged my adolescent heart to worship. With over-use, however (and, my, how we have overused that song!), a once fresh form lost its original power. It grew faded. I could sing it from memory, without thinking in the least about the words I was mouthing. It failed to call me to worship. It no longer provided an effective vehicle for confessing that Jesus "makes his home in my heart." Now, I blush to say, that song is dead to me—worse than dead. It is like fingernails on a chalkboard. It moves me, not to worship, but to homicidal impulses.

To Renovate or Innovate?

All religious forms have a natural life span. Whether it be the songs we sing in worship or the methods we use for evangelism or the means we employ to foster holy living—once fresh and effective forms fade and, eventually, cease to serve the function for which they were originally designed. Some of the forms we inherit from the past continue to be powerful, convicting, effective, and relevant expressions of our religious life; they help us to do what God has called us to do. Some forms, however—with over-use and thoughtless use—have faded and lost their relevance and power. Many of the practices and habits bequeathed to us by the church of our fathers have lost all connection to contemporary minds and hearts. Once-vivid forms, with the passing of time, have become dead ritual and mindless liturgy and instinctive tradition.

When that occurs, what is the church to do? What does faithfulness demand of us in such circumstances? Some of us appear to be arguing that holding to the forms, whether they function or not, is the only true measure of faithfulness. Some seem to be saying that getting the forms right *is* the function of God's people. But the very notion that Jesus would now commend the kind of stubbornness about form that, during his own life, he roundly condemned turns his ministry and message upside down.

Religious forms must always serve religious functions. Faithfulness was (in Jesus' day) and is (today) a matter of functioning as God's people—and finding forms that allow us to do so. The only options left to us—when we recognize that forms have a life span and are always in the process of losing their freshness, effectiveness, relevance and functionality—are either to breathe new life into old forms or to invent new forms that can serve the church effectively. The church must be constantly renovating its forms or innovating new forms that allow it to be God's living presence in this world.

To suggest that fading forms be assigned, willy nilly, to the trash heap would be foolish and unrealistic. There can be no continuity with the past, no heritage to pass on to the future, if we throw away every religious form that begins to look a little ragged around the edges. It is not only possible but desirable to breathe fresh life into older forms. Some ancient songs are worth explaining. Some long-standing ministries are worth reinvigorating. Certain programs and methods and traditions have enough useful life left in them to merit an infusion of renewed understanding and enthusiasm. So long as there are forms close at hand that, with a little attention and encouragement, can continue to help us function as God's people, we ought not look for something new.

Indeed, some forms must not be abandoned or else serious damage will be done to the godly functioning of the church. I agree with Shelley and Harris when they state:

> Two of the continuing marks of the church through all its history are the central rites of baptism and the Lord's Supper . . . . We are convinced that these are instances where theological principles are so enmeshed with their forms that a rejection of the forms entails a significant theological loss.[4]

Both baptism and the Supper are religious forms. They are the practical means by which we enact our spiritual death and resurrection and our dependence on Christ for spiritual sustenance. Like all forms, these too are liable to the kind of habituation that drains them of their significance and their ability to draw our thinking to higher things. All of us have struggled with taking the Supper, week after week, and keeping it as fresh and meaningful and relevant as the first time we gathered at the Lord's table. Those of us who were raised in the church and have seen a hundred baptisms sometimes find it difficult to remember the miracle that is occuring there in the water and in the life of our new brother or sister.

But, at least in the case of these two forms, we are not free to abandon them simply because there are times when they do not function as powerful vehicles for religious commitment. Both forms are so enmeshed with the core of what it means to be a Christian that we must constantly be in the business of "reinvigorating" them—reminding ourselves often of their meaning; refusing to let them degenerate in practice to empty ritual and ceremony; reinforcing the covenant that lies behind the symbol.

But very few of the forms we use entail this degree of theological significance. Most of our forms are helpful to the church only so long as they remain fresh, effective, and relevant vehicles for the purposes we are expected to pursue. When our forms cease to work, when they become rote, when they fail to make the point for which they were designed, when no amount of resuscitation can revive them to former levels of vitality, faithfulness demands that the church value its functions enough to discover new forms by which to express obedience to God.

Howard Snyder is right in making the following observation:

> History teaches...that structures [i.e., forms] will succumb to institutionalism and become hindrances to the gospel rather than helps. The fact that God has raised up a movement is no warranty against eventual infidelity or idolatry. Having clearly distinguished such structures from the essence of the Church, we can freely ask to what extent these forms are actually functioning without fearing we are somehow desecrating holy things.[5]

He recognizes that every form we use to give expression to "the gospel" is susceptible to a kind of deadening that eventually hinders rather than helps the gospel. He also recognizes that movements tend to make idols of their forms, elevating them to the status of "holy things" and failing to make a clear distinction between "the essence of the church" and the means we use to enact the essential. When forced to choose between a dead form and the need to function as God wants, the church should not fear it is desecrating holy things by discarding old forms and adopting new ones. What is holy are the functions to which God has called us. The only desecration we need fear is the disrespect we show to God's eternal purposes by clinging too long and too closely to forms that have ceased to function.

If three points and a poem or careful exegesis of Greek verb tenses fail to call modern audiences to a deeper appreciation of God's word and a fuller obedience to his commands, then we must discover new ways of preaching that accomplish the purposes for which preaching was intended. If the order of our assemblies puts our people to sleep rather than helping them to adore God, we must change the order so that fresh, effective, relevant worship is encouraged. If a seminar on marriage is more likely to draw an audience from our communities than a gospel meeting, if staffing a counseling center makes a greater impact on the world around us than stocking a food pantry, if small groups meeting in homes are more likely to foster intimate fellowship than a pot-luck dinner on Sunday afternoons, we should not fear that we are desecrating holy things by adopting new forms that permit us to be more faithful to old functions.

Much of the controversy that is presently afflicting Churches of Christ—about the way in which we "do" church, involving everything from worship styles to modes of outreach to the substitution of small groups for Wednesday night "prayer meetings"—has little to do with weightier theological matters and much to do with our reluctance to recognize that what worked for our fathers works less well for us and not at all for the generation to follow. We find it difficult to confess that each generation has not only the right but the responsibility to express faith using forms that are timely and effective for it.

There is a life span to religious forms which the church must recognize and address if it is to remain a faithful community of God's people. Form follows function. Faithfulness demands that we be so committed to those divine functions that we employ only those forms that give fresh, effective and relevant expression to them.

Just as—in language—there is an inherent inventiveness that constantly bubbles up fresh metaphors to empower and enliven our speech (sloughing off dead metaphors in favor of newer, more evocative ones), so too—in Christian faith—there is a compelling impetus to discover unconventional forms for refreshed religious expression. That impetus may spring from a desperation to recover a faith for today that is as vigorous as the faith of earlier generations. It may spring from less pure motives: boredom with current practices or envy of the religious experience of others around us. But, at its best, that impetus flows from the desire to revive in modern times the functions and purposes that governed the ancient church. In this sense, it is the advocacy for change and for the discovery of new expressions of faith that represents the true restoration spirit.

Section IV/Toward a Theology of Change

Call me slow. Or perhaps just gullible. But it has taken me a long time to honestly face some of the assumptions that are foundational to our particular enunciation of the Restoration Plea: assumptions about pattern and blueprint and dispensationalism and change, assumptions about what it means to be "faithful" and how to define "obedience," assumptions about the nature of the church and what is central to the task of being God's people.

To tell the truth, my heart knew something was wrong years before my head caught on. I have never been comfortable with the sectarian rhetoric of the "one true church." Our exclusivism and isolationism seemed to me to stem from equal parts arrogance and insecurity. The "identification"

issues that were so critical to others never resonated very strong-
ly with me—probably because I grew up in mission churches
(primarily New Zealand) and was exposed to predominantly
Christ-centered preaching (my father's).

But my concerns had been felt rather than reasoned. I knew
something was amiss, but I could not put my finger on exactly
what and why. It took traveling to Portland, Oregon, and working
with another "mission" congregation (the Westside Church of
Christ), to face squarely the assumptions I no longer believed or, at
least, no longer believed to be important. My experience there
forced me to grapple with hard questions at a conscious, deliberate, theological level.

The result of that struggle has been life to me. Free to return
to the biblical texts and ask questions, I discovered that the
answers I had memorized as a teen were not always in line with the
evidence of God's word. In particular, our conclusions about "pattern" and "change" simply made no sense when viewed through
the lens of Scripture. Many of the constraints under which we
labored as a church—constraints honored because we wanted to
be "faithful"—turned out to be self-imposed rather than God-
imposed, a product of the "fence" we had built around the Bible
rather than the Bible itself.

The chapters you have just read represent an attempt to state
positively and clearly what the Churches of Christ should focus
on— our God-given business. That business involves function, not
form; the ends of the kingdom, not the methods or the means.

Of course, even if we agree that the church should function in
particular ways, important questions still remain: "How do we
express those functions? What forms can we use? Are we free to
create fresh forms? Does the Bible give us permission to change
forms in order to be faithful to our function as God's people?"

These next chapters attempt a partial answer to those questions. Chapter Ten looks at some of the assumptions we have
made about "dispensations" and the process of change. We have

denied the legitimacy of religious changes within dispensations, and supported that denial by reading our Bibles in particular ways. But there is more to the Bible story than we have acknowledged. Chapter Eleven looks at the assumption regarding "pattern" in the early church. The tension between Jewish (Jerusalem) Christianity and Gentile (Antioch) Christianity clearly establishes there never was the "pattern" we have so vehemently asserted. In fact, from the very beginning, churches were doing the "same things differently." And Chapter Twelve addresses the generational struggle over change. Can different generations learn to "sing" together even when their preferences and styles are so disparate?

10/ Change and Time

When Moses descended from Sinai holding the stone tablets in his arms, he brought with him more than the Ten Commandments. There were instructions about annual festivals and the sacrificial system, food laws and laws governing the social life of Israel. There were instructions about the priesthood and the treatment of slaves and personal hygiene.

Most of all, there were specific and detailed instructions about the tabernacle. Large segments of Exodus and Numbers are dedicated to a description of how the tabernacle was to look, how it was to be constructed, what materials were to be used, and how it was to be moved from place to place. According to God's plan, the tabernacle was to be the center of worship for Israel—a large, mobile tent perfectly designed for the needs of a nomadic people who would be on the move for a long time. Far more was said about the tabernacle in the books of Exodus, Leviticus, and Numbers than about circumcision, sacrifices, or the Sabbath day.[1]

Had you been among the Israelites gathered at the foot of Sinai to receive the Law, you would have heard a great deal about the tabernacle. You would have contributed some of the materials that went into building it. You would have heard the command of

God to "Make this tabernacle and all its furnishings exactly like the pattern I will show you" (Ex 25:9). You would have witnessed the final raising of the great tent and seen Moses consecrate it in solemn ceremony (Num 7:1). And you would have seen God's presence come upon the tabernacle, filling it with his glory (Ex. 40:34-35).

You might think that something so important, so minutely commanded, so obviously a matter close to the heart of God would remain an essential part of the religious life of Israel for centuries to come. And you would be right. For 400 years, the tabernacle endured as the center of Israel's religious devotions.

But, then, things changed. By the closing decades of the second millenium before Christ, the Israelites had long been settled in the Promised Land. They were no longer a wandering people. David had conquered Jerusalem and named it the capital city of the land. He had just completed the building of a substantial and luxurious palace to house himself and his harem.

But David found himself in a difficult position. For while he lived in a spanking new palace, God continued to reside in an ancient tent. Embarrassed by the discrepancy, David determined to build a temple for the Lord.

> After the king was settled in his palace and the LORD had given him rest from all his enemies around him, he said to Nathan the prophet, "Here I am, living in a palace of cedar, while the ark of God remains in a tent." Nathan replied to the king, "Whatever you have in mind, go ahead and do it, for the LORD is with you." That night the word of the LORD came to Nathan, saying: "Go and tell my servant David, 'This is what the LORD says: Are you the one to build me a house to dwell in? I have not dwelt in a house from the day I brought the Israelites up out of Egypt to this day. I have been moving from place to place with a tent as my dwelling. Wherever I have moved with

all the Israelites, did I ever say to any of their rulers whom
I commanded to shepherd my people Israel, "Why have
you not built me a house of cedar?"' (2 Sam. 7:1-7).

Scripture makes it clear that the temple was David's idea, not
God's. There was no revelation initiating this matter, no revoking of
the commands given to Moses concerning the tabernacle. There was
only a new situation for the people of God, introducing the need for
a new house of worship. When Solomon finally built the temple—
according to the wishes of his father—it was constructed to different
measurements, built of different materials, furnished with different
treasures, than the specific instructions given by God in Exodus.

And, of course, God rejected this new temple because it was not
according to "the pattern" he had laid down in the book of the Law.

Well, not exactly. In fact, God whole-heartedly endorsed the
efforts of his people to honor him with this house he had not
requested. "When the priests withdrew from the Holy Place, the
cloud filled the temple of the LORD. And the priests could not perform their service because of the cloud, for the glory of the LORD
filled his temple" (1 Kgs. 8:10-11).

After Solomon dedicated the temple with prayer and sacrifices,
the Lord appeared to him and said: "I have heard the prayer and plea
you have made before me; I have consecrated this temple which you
have built, by putting my Name there forever. My eyes and my
heart will always be there" (1 Kgs. 9:3).

Had you been among the Israelites gathered in Jerusalem that
day, you would have seen the glory of the Lord filling the temple.
You would have witnessed the transfer of the sacrifices and priestly
ministrations from the tabernacle to the temple. You would have
taken pride, as Solomon did, in this "magnificent temple" and
prayed with him that God's "eyes be open toward this temple night
and day" (1 Kgs. 8:29).

Again, you might think that something so substantial, so visibly endorsed by Yahweh, would remain an essential part of the

religious life of Israel for centuries to come. And you would be right. For 400 years, the temple endured as the center of Israel's religious devotions.

But, then, once again things changed. Nebuchadnezzar's brutal armies destroyed the temple in 586 B.C. and carried Israel away into captivity. The Ark of the Covenant, the altar of sacrifice, the Holy of Holies—all were annihilated. Israel found herself in a strange land, struggling to relate to her God in a radically changed situation. Without the sacrifices, without the Levitic priesthood, without the Altar and the Holy of Holies, how could Israel worship?

It was during this dark period that, once again, a new situation introduced the need for a new mode of worship. Jews began to gather in small groups throughout Babylon. Lacking priests to guide their devotions, they turned to Rabbis—learned and holy men who, though not related to Aaron, shared his love of God's law. Instead of mass gatherings at the temple for sacrifices and ceremonies, Israelites congregated in homes for informal services during which prayers were uttered, songs were sung, and Scripture was read. In this tentative and evolutionary manner, the worship of the synagogue developed.

Even when the exiles returned to Canaan and rebuilt the temple, even after the sacrifices were again being offered on a consecrated altar, even though the Aaronic priesthood was reestablished to perform its authorized ministry before the Lord—the synagogue remained (and remains to this day) an important and central part of Israel's worship. Having discovered a form of worship which sustained and preserved its devotion to God in difficult circumstances, Israel was reluctant to give up the synagogue even after the temple cultus was reestablished.

And, of course, God rejected this form of worship because it was not according to "the pattern" he had laid down in the book of the Law.

Well—again—not exactly. Though there is no record of a cloud settling on any particular synagogue or the presence of the

Lord filling these gathering places as it did the tabernacle and the temple, there is a record of Jesus endorsing synagogue worship with his presence. Luke states that attendance at synagogue on the Sabbath was Jesus' "custom." He tells us of four specific incidents that took place while Jesus worshipped in a synagogue. And he indicates that Jesus made it a point to preach in the synagogues of Galilee and Judea whenever possible.

Had you been present at the synagogue when Jesus attended, you would have heard him sing and pray with the rest of the congregation. You might have heard him read from Scripture and preach. And you would have been justified in thinking that—though the rituals of the synagogue bore little resemblance to the worship prescribed in the Law—Jesus believed God could be worshipped as well from a synagogue as from a tabernacle.

A Dispensationalist's Guide to History

Those of us whose roots run deep in the soil of the American Restoration Movement have developed a way of reading Scripture that taps into the strict assumptions of dispensationalism. Oh, we don't often use the term "dispensations," but the notion shapes our thinking whether or not we know what to call it. We more commonly speak of "ages"—as in the Patriarchical Age, the Mosaic Age, the Christian Age.

Whatever the terms used, the idea is that religious life and practice consists of long and essentially static "eras," punctuated by rare but revolutionary upheavals in the ways people and God relate to each other. The simple and unstructured worship of Abraham, Isaac, and Jacob was sufficient for many centuries. But, eventually, it was replaced by the ordered and priest-dependent cultus of Moses and Aaron—a religious, social, and moral system which held sway for almost 1500 years. The time came, however, when Jesus "canceled the written code... he took it away, nailing it to the cross" and even Moses had to yield to the new covenant and the worship of the New Testament church.

There is much to commend a dispensational view of religious history. Anyone familiar with the Bible can easily recognize differences between God's covenants with Abraham, Moses and Christ. But there are two assumptions flowing out of this viewpoint that, taken together, have been problematic for those of us in the Restoration Movement.

The first assumption is that legitimate religious change occurs between dispensations—when a new lawgiver emerges to mediate a new covenant based on new revelation. An intentional, God-initiated tear in the fabric of human history justifies any modifications in the way we worship and live out our religious lives. Moses and Jesus introduced radical changes (indeed, established essentially new religions), but they did so as the specially anointed agents of God, bringing with them a new covenant between God and his people. Revolution is permissible between the dispensations because it is founded in revelation. It is ordained by God.

To assume that a new "age" was instituted by Jesus and that the changes initiated by him were legitimate because they flowed from a fresh revelation of God's will is foundational for the Christian faith. On what other basis could the early church justify a break from Judaism or Paul argue for a "righteousness apart from the Law" except that, with the coming of Jesus, the rules had been radically rewritten? The language of Hebrews (regarding a "better covenant" and a "better priest" and the Law being "only a shadow of the good things to come") would be nonsense apart from the conviction that God broke into history with Jesus Christ and ushered a new dispensation into existence.

It's not our acceptance of "rare but revolutionary upheavals" in religious history that has tripped us up, but the corollary assumption of "long and essentially static eras" in between. We have tended to see the millennia from Abraham to Moses, from Moses to Christ, and from Christ until the present time as religiously fixed periods—frozen epochs stretching between brief avalanches of religious change. Abraham, Moses, and Christ had the authority to initiate change. Living within the dispensations they introduced, however, means living within the new constraints they established.

This second assumption—that changes initiated within a dispensation are illegitimate—flows understandably from the first. Evolution in religious life and practice during a particular dispensation cannot be permitted. Once God breaks into history with a new covenant, a pattern is set that must be honored and strictly adhered to by all those who want to be faithful. Someone living in the Mosaic Age, for example—whether a contemporary of Moses or Samuel or Nehemiah—was bound to follow exactly the terms of the covenant delivered at Sinai, because, once set in "stone," the established pattern could not be altered without incurring the displeasure of God.[2]

If you will forgive the analogy, history seen from a dispensational perspective has God and humanity engaged in an extended session of poker. On rare occasions, the divine Dealer will call for a change of game (say, from five card draw to seven card stud) and the faithful must adjust themselves to the new set of rules which apply. What we cannot do is initiate any changes in the game ourselves. Once the game is set, we are required to follow the new rules that have been established.

In the absence of new revelation, what possible justification for religious change can be made? Certainly, changing conditions and circumstances might suggest changes in worship and lifestyle. The passing of time and the vagaries of human culture may call for pragmatic responses. Reasonable people who are sincerely seeking, in a fickle world, to remain faithful to a changeless God may initiate well-intentioned alterations. But, however, you cut it, such changes are the result of human judgment rather than divine proclamation.

Because we do not trust "human judgment" to make such changes wisely and with the guidance of the Spirit, we are forced to regard any change as a dangerous "innovation" leading down the slippery slope to apostasy. In a single stroke, we disallow the possibility of legitimate change within a dispensation, opting instead for those "long and essentially static eras" where change is not only suspect, it is heretical.

Restoration and Change

It is easy to see how these assumptions have shaped our particular enunciation of the restoration plea. The "pattern" for Christian worship, church structure, ministry, and lifestyle was established 2000 years ago when Jesus and the apostles received a new revelation and instituted a new set of rules governing the interaction between God and human beings. The revolutionary changes which were involved were legitimate because they were divinely ordained.

What we see in the New Testament church is the first implementation of a Christian pattern for a Christian dispensation. Though not perfect, this early example becomes binding for all later Christians (or so the logic goes) because, once the pattern is established, it cannot be legitimately altered. The task of the faithful Christian living now in the Christian era is to carefully replicate the pattern found in the New Testament across cultures and centuries. Subsequent changes to the initial pattern, no matter how "reasonable" or well-intended or minor, are heretical because they are rooted not in fresh revelation but in the flawed and limited understanding of mere men.

In order to bolster this second assumption—that changes within dispensations are illegitimate—we have turned to the Old Testament to find instructive parallels. If it can be demonstrated that changes to the Mosaic pattern met with divine displeasure, one could logically assume that changes to the Christian pattern would meet with similar disapproval.

And so we have searched the Old Testament, looking for evidence of "long and essentially static" religious periods where change was synonymous with unfaithfulness and the same rules adhered over centuries of time. We have selectively culled stories from the biblical record that underscored our dispensational views and used them to emphasize the illegitimacy of religious change apart from a divine initiative. Nadab and Abihu became the particular hammer we used to drive this point home. Because they deviated from the pattern for worship in the tabernacle when they offered "strange fire," they had to pay for their innovation with their lives.[3] The moral to that story is simple: once the pattern is set, it must be strictly followed, without addition or subtraction, in order to be pleasing to God.

By implication, this reading of the Old Testament has persuaded us that every detail of the behavior of the New Testament church must be paradigmatic for the twentieth-century church's attempts to worship and serve and live out the Christian lifestyle. Since the pattern was established by Jesus and his apostles (the only "change agents" we recognize as legitimate), and since subsequent changes to that pattern represent changes within the Christian dispensation and without direct revelation, the task of the faithful is to keep the pattern exactly or restore it when it has been altered. Indeed, innovations must be labeled for what we believe them to be—misguided efforts to offer "strange fire" that is contrary to the specific instructions of God and the explicit example of the early church.

The Rest of the Story

But what if our reading of the Old Testament has been skewed? What if the "essentially static" dispensation we have searched for does not exist—at least to the degree we have claimed? The stark transition from tabernacle to temple to synagogue calls into question our assumption that, once a pattern was established under Moses, no changes were allowed. I'll bet you have never heard a single sermon that addressed this transition and God's adoption of these unauthorized changes to accomplish his will. Yet not one word of rebuke or chastisement for these "innovations" is recorded in Scripture. They represent radical alterations to the specifically commanded pattern established by God on Sinai. But God not only endured them, he embraced them and wrote them into his script for dealing with his people. How can that be if, once the pattern is established, it is to be held inviolate until a new dispensation with new rules is revealed?

Nor is this an isolated example—an exception which proves the rule. The same kind of evolution of religious life within the Mosaic age can be demonstrated in other ways. How could God possibly countenance Israel's selection of a king? Here is a case of a change that was not simply unauthorized by God but contrary to God's expressed will. As early as Deuteronomy, God had predicted that Israel would ask for a king (Deut. 17:14ff). But when, in the days of Samuel, the request is made by the people, God makes it plain that their demand is a repudiation of his own leadership of Israel.

> So all the elders of Israel gathered together and came to Samuel at Ramah. They said to him, "You are old, and your sons do not walk in your ways; now appoint a king to lead us, such as all the other nations have." But when they said, "Give us a king to lead us," this displeased Samuel; so he prayed to the LORD. And the LORD told him: "Listen to all that the people are saying to you; it is not you they have rejected, but they have rejected me as their king. As they have done from the day I brought them up out of Egypt until this day, forsaking me and serving other gods, so they are doing to you (1 Sam 8:4-8).

Here is an example of a religious innovation (for all of Israel's life was "religious" in that it was governed and directed by God) that is rooted in open rebellion and disobedience. The request for a king was a bald accommodation to secular culture—"We want a king over us. Then we will be like all the other nations, with a king to lead us and go out before us and fight our battles" (1 Sam. 8:19-20). Samuel refers to this request as "an evil thing" (1 Sam. 12:17).

Yet God embraces this change as well. It wasn't that God yielded grudgingly to this departure from his covenant or worked around this human impediment to accomplish his will. By establishing a monarchy in Israel, God was able to set David on the throne and pave the way (through his dynasty) for the coming of the Messiah. Israel's king became the centerpiece of God's efforts to predict, define, and bring into existence the "anointed one." God was able to take Israel's demand for a king and turn it, eventually, into the "King of kings."

The tabernacle-temple-synagogue movement and the transition from prophet to judge to king are only the two most sweeping examples of a reality of Old Testament life. The Mosaic Age was not nearly so static and unchanging as we have imagined. And the God of the Mosaic Age was not nearly so unaccommodating of change as we have painted him to be.

The truth of the matter is that, within the period governed by the Mosaic Law, there were significant changes occurring in the life and worship of Israel. When conditions required it, when Israel found herself in situations not envisioned or covered by the terms of her covenant with God, when the times demanded it, religious changes were made. Some were well-intentioned and some were sheer rebellion. Some were volunteered by Israel and some were forced upon her. Some were prompted by changing circumstances and some were the result of Israel's fickle affections. These changes were not initiated by fresh revelation or even a closer reading of Israel's sacred texts. They were pragmatic responses to the passing of time and new challenges presented to God's people.

Yet, often if not always, God found a way to sanction these changes and use them to further his purposes. Not all religious changes were repudiated by Yahweh. It was possible, under the Law, to adapt and adjust and acclimate and still be pleasing to God. It is simply not true that the only legitimate changes in Israel's relationship to God occurred on Mount Sinai. Some legitimate and necessary changes occurred hundreds of years later and many miles removed from that wilderness mountain. When all is said and done, it was better for Israel to worship in a synagogue than refuse to worship at all without the divinely sanctioned accouterments of the tabernacle. It was better for Israel to have a king than for "every man to do what was right in his own eyes."

Re-reading our Bibles

There is a great deal of talk about "change" among the Churches of Christ today, but precious little effort to develop a "theology of change." Proponents of both sides of the debate dig their positional trenches and hurl charges and counter-charges at each other, but what they hurl has as much to do with ossified traditions or the latest church growth fads as it does with Scripture.

The only starting point we can trust for this ongoing discussion of our future is the Bible. It is clear to me that a fresh reading of Scripture is needed among us. Perhaps we should be talking a little less and reading a little more.

But in order to read *faithfully*, we will have to read differently. It is not respectful of Scripture to begin with a restoration ethic ("We must restore the pattern that was first exemplified in the early church"), based on a certain view of change ("The only legitimate changes occur at the beginning of a dispensation; changes within dispensations are heretical"), and then read our Bibles to find evidence that supports such a view. That sort of biased approach to Scripture has done great damage to us theologically, and promoted our assumptions about biblical texts above the evidence of the texts themselves.

There were profound changes that occurred between the time of Moses and the coming of Christ. The Old Testament provides examples at every turn, if only we are willing to read with fresh eyes. Many of these changes were endorsed by God and incorporated in his salvation plan. A more careful reading of these texts— one that begins with the texts themselves—allows a theology of change to develop from them, and then determines whether or what sort of restorationists we should be—what sort is necessary if we are to be faithful readers.

I am convinced that a re-reading of the Bible will challenge our assumptions about change. It will challenge the dispensational framework that leads us to dismiss all changes within a particular "age" as heretical. It will call us to think more carefully about how circumstance and culture and time impact the people of God and demand adaptations of them. It will require that we delve into questions about motive and wisdom and how the Spirit of God works to guide human reason to accomplish divine ends.

Rather than reading our Bibles in such a way as to rule out the legitimacy of change, we should be looking for why some changes were approved while others were not. What was it about the hearts and intentions of Old Testament "innovators" that resulted at one time in blessing and at another in curses? Why did God embrace certain modifications of his expressed will, while absolutely and vehemently damning others? Is it possible that God permits, even encourages, changes to the "letter of the law" when circumstances require such changes in order to keep the "spirit of the law"? Might it be that ignoring the "spirit" makes keeping or changing the "letter" equally repugnant to God?

It seems evident that all this has radical implications for our understanding of "restoration." If the task of the modern church is somehow "other" than to restore in pristine fashion the pattern of worship and ministry expressed by the New Testament church, if changing circumstances legitimate in our day the same kinds of religious changes we read about in David's or Daniel's day, then in what way can we claim to be "restorationists"? As you have already seen, I still believe that we are called to restore today something that we see in the first-century church. But what exactly does God want us to revive?

We ought to remember that it was the fervent restorationists of the Mosaic Age who crucified Jesus. The Pharisees were interested in nothing so much as restoring to first-century Judaism the clear pattern of Sinai. They wore the required clothing when no one else would. They kept the food laws. They were meticulous about the Sabbath Day. They eschewed the religious changes and adaptations that had accumulated through the centuries. In every way possible, they attempted to bring contemporary Israel into line with the ancient covenant. (Although, it is interesting that even they were not calling for a return to the tabernacle. The Pharisees were quite comfortable with the temple and the synagogue!)

But they were restoring the wrong things. Was God most interested in Israel's costume or her character? Was his concern for what went into her (what Israel ate) or what came out of her? Was his intent to restore the Sabbath Day or to identify the Lord of the Sabbath? While the Pharisees were busy with God's pattern, they missed entirely God's person.

It is a problem with which we modern restorationists can identify all too easily.

In the following chapter, we will see that the necessity of change is evidenced not only across the centuries from Moses to Christ but across the varied cultures in which the gospel of Jesus was preached. Israel had no monopoly on changes that could be endorsed and exploited by God. The early church was equally adept at adapting to changing circumstances and situations.

Dear Joseph,

Just a quick note about the recent Jerusalem conference on the "Gentile Question." Since you live among the pagans, I thought you might want to know what happened.

"The Gentiles must be circumcised and required to obey the Law." It is an obvious statement of truth. God gave the Law and intends it to be obeyed. Certainly, we Jews have found it difficult to keep the Law perfectly. But just because it is difficult does not mean it can be abandoned!

And, yes, the Gentiles will have a hard time obeying Moses' laws: eating only kosher foods, making the pilgrimages, learning the sacrificial system. But those who are truly dedicated, who really love God and want to do what is right, will find a way to learn and comply with God's eternal commands.

The conference was called, of course, because some were arguing a radical position—in every group there have to be a few liberals. They wanted to require nothing more of Gentiles than that they believe in Christ and abstain from sin. They actually thought it was possible to please God without obedience to his specifically commanded will! They argued that Jewish Christians should accept and have fellowship with Gentile Christians who were not circumcised, who did not keep the Sabbath, and who did not keep a Kosher table! As if there could be two standards by which discipleship was measured—one for the serious, Jewish Christian and one for the worldly, uncommitted heathens.

It was a good thing that some strong, faithful men stood up and insisted that what was good for us was good for everyone who wanted to be a Christian. A letter has been written to all Gentile Christians insisting that they be circumcised and follow the commands of Moses as well as those of Christ. After all, even our Lord said that he had not come to abolish the law but to fulfill it. That is all we are asking Gentile Christians to do.

This will obviously limit your audience among the Gentiles. Few of them love God enough to take on the burden that we more dedicated and obedient disciples are carrying. But remember that the way is hard and the door is narrow—as our Lord said, "Few there are who find it."

So, Joseph, make sure that you keep everything Yahweh has commanded in the Law and the prophets. Those who love Jesus obey the commands of his Father. And make sure that you teach those pagans you allow into the church to keep everything in the Law. I know it is tempting to slack up on them, but you do them no favors by sparing them from the full call to discipleship.

An obedient servant of the God who is the same yesterday, today, and forever,

A Concerned Pharisee.

11/ Change and Culture

Imagine how different the course of Christian history would have been had the Jerusalem Conference (Acts 15) taken a different turn! Luke makes it clear (both from the account of the conference itself and as subsequent events unfold) that there were many at that conference pushing the proposition, "The Gentiles must be circumcised and required to obey the Law of Moses" (Acts 15:5). Their arguments were reasonable, their worries were real, their intentions were good. But they were wrong.

Underlying the debate of Acts 15 was the assumption that a common commitment to Christ should result in common religious practice. The Christians of Jerusalem could not imagine condoning and fellowshipping a brand of Gentile Christianity that differed significantly from the Christianity practiced in Jerusalem. What was good for Jewish Christians in Judea ought to be good for Gentile Christians throughout the Mediterranean world. The realities of diverse people and cultures could only be accommodated by a single, unified practice of Christian life and worship—or so the thinking went.

These Jewish Christians were the first "patternists" of the Christian faith. They had discovered—in those early, innocent years of the church in Jerusalem—a pattern for worshipping God "according to the Way." They had established particular forms (many borrowed from the Judaism of the day) through which they expressed their life before God and their devotion to his Son. They would have gladly, contentedly, lived out their lives practicing this brand of nascent Christianity and mutant Judaism had it not been for those pesky Gentiles.

Now, faced with a flood of Gentile converts who threatened to overwhelm the Jewish core of the church with their different languages and cultures and habits and mores, the Christians of Jerusalem found themselves wrestling with the question, "Do Gentiles have to express their life before God in the same manner as we Jews?" It is similar to the question being asked among Churches of Christ today: "Do we have to express our life before God using the same forms and practices as the church two thousand (or even thirty) years ago?" For many—then in Jerusalem and now in the church—the answer is a resounding, "Yes!"

A Brief Look at the Jerusalem Church

The birth of the Jerusalem church occurred on Pentecost, 50 days after the death of Jesus. And for the next five years, the Christian message did not wander far from the womb. The church in Jerusalem enjoyed an incubation period during which forms of worship, structures for community, patterns for evangelism, etc. could be developed. During this time, there were no churches in Gentile territory, no churches in Galilee or Samaria, no other churches at all. There was only one way to "do church" because there was only one church. The Jerusalem church was *it*.

And what kind of church was it? It was a congregation shaped as much by Moses and the customs of Israel as by Christ. It was made up exclusively of Jews—no Gentiles need apply. They continued to circumcise their children, to observe kosher food laws, and to pray at the appointed hours. They kept the Sabbath and felt perfectly comfortable gathering in the synagogue with their Jewish brothers one day and in the temple courts with their Jewish/Christian brothers the next. They purified themselves according to the traditions of their fathers. They persisted in taking distinctly Jewish vows. They wore the fringes and phylacteries prescribed by the Law. In all probability, they continued to offer sacrifices on the altar of the temple even as they learned to offer their whole lives in sacrifice to Christ.

When they gathered to worship, they met at the temple, in Solomon's Colonnade. Nor was this a small group, huddling in the corner to softly sing *Kumbiyah*. Thousands of Christians came there daily for worship and instruction. If you pause to wonder why, over such a long period, the temple authorities did not grow more concerned about what was happening right under their noses, one simple answer is that Jewish-Christian worship was virtually indistinguishable from the worship of orthodox Judaism. No doubt, early Christians sang the songs of their fathers, using the words of David and the melodies with which they had all been raised. The Scriptures they quoted were from the Jewish canon. Their preachers spoke Aramaic and used the rhetorical conventions of the rabbis.

Most of all, when they spoke of Jesus, they spoke in terms easily understood by their Jewish countrymen. Jesus was the Messiah, the promised one, the seed of David, the deliverer of Israel. Though non-Christian Jews may have quibbled with *whether* Jesus was the Messiah, most would have been perfectly comfortable with the language, scriptures and hope that suffused the Apostles' message concerning the Christ.

When, at last, God forced the hand of the Jerusalem church and scattered those first Christians abroad, they "preached the word wherever they went" (Acts 8:4). But not to whomever they met. The gospel was still a distinctly Jewish privilege and preaching was aimed exclusively at Jewish (or proselyte) audiences (see Acts 11:19). As a result, it was quite natural for Jerusalem Christians to export not only the message of salvation through Jesus Christ but also the manner in which they were "doing church." With only the slightest modifications, Jews in Samaria or Phoenicia or Cyprus could join their Jerusalem brothers in a common practice of their common new faith. They had not yet been forced to question whether it was really necessary to be a good Jew in order to be a good Christian.

Not, that is, until Gentiles came on the scene. The first storm-cloud on the horizon did not blow in until some seven or eight years after the church began in Jerusalem. Peter made his fateful journey to Caesarea (A.D. 37 or 38?) and baptized a Gentile. The complaint made by his Jewish brothers was ostensibly about fraternizing with Gentiles and having table-fellowship with them. The real issue, though, was whether Gentiles could become Christians at all. It took a three-fold vision from God and a dramatic outpouring of the Spirit to win from Peter the grudging concession, "Who was I to think that I could oppose God?" and from the Jewish Christians an acknowledgment that even Gentiles could experience "repentance unto life" (Acts 11:17-18).

A Brief Look at the Antioch Church

Of course, knowing what to do with Gentiles once they *became* Christians was another matter altogether. About the same time that Peter was working with Cornelius (sometime in the late 30s), other evangelists had made their circuitous way through Northern Africa and the island of Cyprus to Antioch in Syria. Unintentionally, almost accidentally, they would have the privilege of forcing the gospel cat out of the Jewish bag.

Luke tells us (see Acts 11) that certain Jews began "to speak to Greeks also, telling them the good news about the Lord Jesus." More to the point, the Greeks listened eagerly and responded to the message in "great numbers." Before anyone realized what was happening, before anyone had thought through the consequences of what they were doing, a new kind of church came into existence, populated almost entirely by Gentiles. When Jerusalem (a year or two later) heard what was happening,. the Apostles sent Barnabas to Antioch. One look at the church there and Barnabas went searching for Saul of Tarsus. That following year (A.D. 42/43?) saw phenomenal growth in the Antioch church and fundamental changes in the practice of the Christian faith.

The Antioch church was as Gentile as the Jerusalem church was Jewish. The Christians of Antioch spoke a different language, had been shaped by a different culture, lived a different ethic and lifestyle, had a completely different set of problems and priorities. In Jerusalem, followers of Jesus were known as "the believers" or members of "the Way" (Acts 1:15; 2:44; 4:32; 5:12; 9:2); but in Antioch, they were called "Christians" (Acts 11:26). They did not circumcise their children (or themselves) when they accepted Jesus. They paid little or no attention to Jewish ways and customs. In this church, we have the first specific record of kosher food laws being ignored, not only by the Gentiles who had never observed such restrictions but also by the Jewish Christians who were teaching these Gentiles about the Lord (Gal. 2:11ff).

They had to formulate Christian responses to problems Jerusalem Christians could not have imagined. How were Gentile Christians (for instance) to interact with a culture saturated in idolatry? Could they attend meetings at local temples (common gathering sites for both business and social appointments)? Could they go to the market and buy meat that had been used in pagan sacrifices? What sort of relationship were they to have with their idolatrous neighbors? Such questions, unimaginable in Jerusalem, were of critical importance for the Antioch church. The answers to such questions shaped the life of Antioch Christians in very different directions from their Jerusalem brethren.

Though we are told little about the manner in which the Antioch church worshipped, it is safe to assume that the forms used to express worship were drawn from their native culture rather than a Jewish one. They didn't meet in the temple or even in synagogues. They probably did not recite the *shema*

(Deut. 6:4-9—"Hear O Israel: The Lord our God, the Lord is one..."), or sing the Ascent Psalms to Hebraic harmonies. Sermons must have been influenced more by Syrian (or even Greek) rhetorical styles than by rabbinical models.

Even when they spoke of Jesus, at the core of their shared faith with churches in Judea and Samaria, it was not messianic themes that were stressed but the idea of Jesus as Savior and Son of God— notions much more accessible by the Syrian mind than arcane, apocalyptic concepts rooted deep in Israel's history.

Now, for the first time, there were two kinds of Christian churches in existence: the Jewish church epitomized by Jerusalem; and the Gentile church found in Antioch. One Lord, one God, one body, one faith held in common. But very different expressions and forms; a great diversity in practice. This tension between Jerusalem and Antioch bounced along for a number of years. Paul and Barnabas set out on their first missionary journey, compounding the problem by establishing more churches throughout Asia Minor with the same sensitivity to local cultures and the same disregard for the Jerusalem pattern. There were serious and fundamental issues bubbling just below the surface, unanswered questions ready to erupt into heated debate.

The Clash

It was not until the mid-40s A.D. (five years after the first converts in Antioch, and 15 years after the birth of the Jerusalem church) that the tension finally became unbearable and the diversity between Jewish and Gentile churches was openly addressed. According to Luke: "Some men came down from Judea to Antioch and were teaching the brothers: 'Unless you are circumcised, according to the custom taught by Moses, you cannot be saved'" (Acts 15:1).

After years of looking to the North and agonizing about what to do with Gentiles once they became Christians, certain Jerusalem Christians had finally found an answer: Gentile Christians had to practice their faith in the same way that Jewish Christians did.

Although it is easy to misunderstand this position as primarily a defense of Judaism, above all it constituted a defense of *Jewish Christianity*. It was not enough for Gentiles to confess Jesus and accept him as Lord. They had to *express* their faith in the same way, using the same forms, following the same customs, as their Jewish brethren.

In effect, this bombshell from Judea meant that in order to be a good Christian, one had to become a practicing Jew. There was to be no such thing as a Gentile Christianity expressed in uniquely Gentile ways. Gentiles had to be circumcised (Acts 15:1), taught to keep the law (15:5), and required to observe Jewish customs (Gal. 2:14). Only in this way could they be "saved." Only in this way could Jewish Christians conscientiously have fellowship with their Gentile brethren. Only in this way could the common faith forge for such diverse people a common and unifying practice.

In Luke's understated language, this brought Paul and Barnabas "into no small dispute and debate" with their Jewish brothers. Paul had already determined that it was possible to function as a Christian without being tied to the forms characteristic either of Judaism or of Jerusalem Christianity. His years in Arabia, Damascus, and—ultimately—in Antioch had convinced him that the gospel that would save and sanctify Gentiles had nothing to do with inculcating the customs of Moses—even if those customs had been baptized by the Jerusalem church and borrowed to serve Christian purposes.

By the time these Jewish Christians came to Antioch, insisting that the Antioch church should follow the Jerusalem pattern, Paul was ready to lay out the core of the gospel he had received from God and preached to Gentiles. How could Gentiles be good Christians? By coming into relationship with Jesus Christ through faith, by being crucified with Jesus, by putting on the new man in place of the old. Period. Paul would not require them to keep the law; he would not insist that they adopt the habits and practices of their Jerusalem brothers; he would not demand a uniformity of practice between the Jewish church and the Gentile one.

Jews could express their relationship to Jesus in Jewish ways. Gentiles could express their walk with Jesus in Gentile ways. The common faith—far from demanding cookie-cutter churches—encouraged diverse practices in diverse situations. There was available in Christ the freedom to express devotion through native idioms and indigenous customs.

When the controversy in Antioch was followed swiftly by the conference in Jerusalem, the leaders of the Jerusalem church publicly affirmed Paul's understanding of the gospel. James spoke for them all in concluding: "It is my judgment that we should not make it difficult for the Gentiles who are turning to God" (Acts 15:19). The letter, sent to "the Gentile believers in Antioch," made the same point:

> It seemed good to the Holy Spirit and to us not to burden you with anything beyond the following requirements: You are to abstain from food sacrificed to idols, from blood, from the meat of strangled animals and from sexual immorality. You will do well to avoid these things. Farewell (Acts 15:28-29).

It is important not to miss the significance of this statement. James and his associates were legitimating different expressions of the Christian faith, given different people and cultures. Plainly, Jerusalem Christians were determined to live by a different standard than that which would be required of Christians in Antioch. They would continue worshipping Christ like Jews, circumcising their children and obeying the law. The Jerusalem conference did not forbid such practices to the Jewish church. It simply refused to let Jerusalem bind those practices on Gentile churches. A Christianity heavily conditioned by Judaism might be justifiable (even necessary) in the capital city of the Jews. But insisting on that same kind of

Christianity in the cities of Syria, Greece or Italy would lead to a stunting of church growth and an abuse of Christian liberty.

The apostles and elders of Jerusalem were stating—for the record—that it was possible for Christianity to take different forms given different audiences. The Gentiles would not be held to a Jerusalem standard. They were free to practice Christianity in culturally appropriate ways.

Of course, not all Jewish Christians agreed with the decision of their leaders. "Judaizers" (whose agenda, if not supervision, came from stubborn elements of the Jerusalem church) intentionally dogged the steps of Paul over the following decade to undermine his work among the Gentiles. "Paul is not telling you the whole story," they would insist. "The true faith is practiced in Jerusalem where the church was first established; where the eye-witnesses of our Lord live; where the true apostles, appointed by the hand of Christ himself, direct the affairs of the church. If you want to be a Christian, you must conform to the Jerusalem pattern." In spite of the "official position," Judaizers caused great damage in the early church by insisting to Gentile Christians that the Jerusalem church was the yardstick by which all other churches would be measured. Their determined efforts indicate that the statement of the Jerusalem leaders—while on the record—was considered off the mark by many Jewish Christians.

A Postscript

Almost ten years after the conference in Jerusalem, Paul returned to the city at the conclusion of his third missionary journey. Luke's account of this final visit (Acts 21) gives us an interesting insight into the enduring Jewish character of the Jerusalem church.

> When we arrived at Jerusalem, the brothers received us warmly. The next day Paul and the rest of us went to see James, and all the elders were present. Then they said to Paul: "You see, brother, how many thousands of Jews have

believed, and all of them are zealous for the law. They have been informed that you teach all the Jews who live among the Gentiles to turn away from Moses, telling them not to circumcise their children or live according to our customs. What shall we do? They will certainly hear that you have come, so do what we tell you. There are four men with us who have made a vow. Take these men, join in their purification rites and pay their expenses, so that they can have their heads shaved. Then everybody will know there is no truth in these reports about you, but that you yourself are living in obedience to the law. As for the Gentile believers, we have written to them our decision that they should abstain from food sacrificed to idols, from blood, from the meat of strangled animals and from sexual immorality" (Acts 21:17-26).

This is an amazing passage! The gospel of Christ had met with great success in Jerusalem—thousands were believers. Yet the one characteristic that James and the elders of the church were quick to emphasize for Paul was the Jerusalem church's zeal for the law. Why? It was not that these Christians had a deficient love for Christ or that other aspects of their Christian walk paled in comparison to their love of Moses. It was, rather, that—in the context of what had been heard about Paul and his ministry—Paul needed to be warned that Jewish Christians were unhappy with the way he was treating their heritage.

Word had come to Jerusalem—the elders themselves were shocked and gave the reports no credence—that Paul did not live like a good Jew when among the Gentiles, telling other Diaspora Jews that, as Christians, they were not obligated to keep the law. Some in the Jerusalem church, foolishly believing such reports, were quite upset with Paul. ("What shall we do? They will certainly hear that you have come.") The implication is clear—had the elders believed those reports themselves, they too would have been upset with Paul.

Paul, of course, was doing precisely what had been reported. Not only had he consistently refused to bind Moses on Gentiles; he encouraged other Jews to do what he himself had done— become "all things to all men so that by all possible means I might save some" (1 Cor. 9:19-22). When Paul's Jewishness got in the way of effectively reaching Gentiles, he gladly set it aside. His consistent encouragement to other Jews working with Gentiles was to do the same. For the "Apostle to the Gentiles," the functions of the kingdom always superseded the forms of Jewish Christianity. When Christian Jews found themselves living in a Gentile world, inappropriate forms had to be jettisoned in favor of new forms that permitted effective functioning. To use Paul's words, "Neither circumcision nor uncircumcision means anything; what counts is a new creation" (Gal. 6:15).

James and the elders of Jerusalem (to their credit) remained committed to the decision made years ago about the Gentiles. Gentiles would still be permitted to practice a different "brand" of Christianity than Jerusalem Jews. What they had failed to understand, however—being isolated both from the Gentile church and from the unique situation of Christian Jews in Gentile territory— was that the same freedom given to Gentiles throughout the Mediterranean world had to be extended to those Jews who lived among them. Evidently, they were under the impression that Jewish Christians would naturally continue to live out the traditions of their fathers, even if they lived in Antioch or Rome. That Paul had abandoned Jewish customs and would advocate that other Jews do so was unthinkable. Hence, they recommended a course of action to Paul that would demonstrate to the Jerusalem church that there was "no truth to these reports" and that he himself "lived in obedience to the law."

Thus, there seem to be three schools of thought regarding how to "do church" in the first-century. The first (epitomized by the Judaizers, including many in the Jerusalem church) was that all Christians everywhere, whatever their background or culture, ought to conduct themselves according to the pattern of the Jerusalem church. The second (represented by James and the elders of Jerusalem) was that all *Jewish* Christians, no matter where they happened to be living, ought to conform themselves to the Jerusalem pattern, while Gentile Christians were free to practice their faith in whatever manner was appropriate and effective in their environment. The third (advocated by Paul) was that all Christians, whatever their background, were free (indeed, required!) to "do church" in ways that were appropriate for their setting and effective for expressing the functions to which God has called his church.

An Epilogue

Within one hundred and fifty years, Jewish Christianity would be labeled as heretical by the church at large. There were no Jewish Christians in Jerusalem then, because there was no Jerusalem. Destroyed in A.D. 70 and again in A.D. 135, a new city—*Aelia Capitolina*—was erected on the ruins of ancient Jerusalem, and all Jews were banned from its precincts.

Eusebius reports that, warned by a prophecy, the church fled Jerusalem *en masse* in A.D. 66, just as the Jewish Wars began. A Jewish/Christian sect known as the *Ebionites* grew up during this period. They demanded faithful adherence to the law, attacked the teachings of Paul, and viewed Jesus primarily as the Messiah who had come to save Israel. In these ways, they differed little from many of the first Jewish believers who populated the church in Jerusalem. The primary differences between this sect and the rest of second-century Christianity was that, while contact with other cultures and ideas forced the rest of Christianity to grow and adapt, the Ebionites remained isolated and insulated, clinging to the old ways and refusing to adapt at all. This sect represented a stunted Christianity, rigid and incapable of speaking the gospel to a changing world. The church of the second and third-century would not tolerate such inflexibility and labeled it "heresy."

Conclusion

To people such as myself—long rooted in notions that there are "patterns" to be discerned and respected regarding the New Testament church, that those patterns had to do primarily with forms and structures and how church "business" was conducted, that what one church did *all* churches must have done because they all followed the same blueprint—the revelation that there was diversity of practice in the New Testament church comes as a shock. On reflection, it is obvious that first-century churches did the same things differently—that Christians in Antioch observed the same faith as Christians in Jerusalem but using different methods and practices. Charismatic Corinthians and esoteric Ephesians would add even more wrinkles to the mix. There were no cookie-cutter churches just as there were no cookie-cutter Christians.

But we haven't reflected on this. Just the opposite. Having made an assumption about uniformity of practice in the early church—an assumption rooted far more in the theological debates of modern times than in the texts we claim to honor—it has been easy for us to define "restoration" as strictly following today the pattern we "discovered" in the ancient church.

To use the language of prior chapters in this book, we have understood the business of restoration to involve particular *forms*, rather than focusing on a modern-day restoration of underlying *functions*. While we could have taken a hint from the clear diversity of New Testament congregations that their (and our) commonalities must be rooted in something deeper than a slavish adherence to similar practices, we did violence to Scriptures—imposing on them (and ourselves) a pattern for practice that existed nowhere but in our own imagination.

In the end, we found ourselves playing Jerusalem to everyone else's Antioch. There was only one way to "do church"—i.e., the manner in which *we* did it. *We* practiced the approved pattern whereby God was honored and the faithful were identified. The forms of worship, fellowship, witness, and holiness *we* employed were required of all churches, no matter their circumstances or background.

In order to please God, all churches must do the same things in basically the same ways. "The Gentiles must be circumcised and required to obey the law of Moses." It's the Judaizers all over again.

I bet Paul's response would be the same now as then. "You don't have to do church like Jerusalem to be saved. You aren't required to adopt the forms that worked so well in rural congregations of the Churches of Christ in the first half of the twentieth-century to be pleasing to God. God's people are called to worship, build community, make disciples, and lead holy lives. God's people must witness to and make a difference in their world. The church must be the aroma of Christ. *How* you do those things, what forms you adopt, what means you use, must be determined by the times and circumstances in which you live. The forms change. The functions never do. Now stop harping on circumcision and get on with the business of the kingdom!"

I will exalt you, my God the King;

  I will praise your name forever and ever.

Every day I will praise you

  and extol your name forever and ever.

Great is the Lord and most worthy of praise;

  his greatness no one can fathom.

Psalm 145:3

12/ A God for All Generations

It is one thing to say that legitimate religious changes can occur with changing time and culture. It is one thing to say that God accommodates to and (on occasion) embraces such changes. It is something else entirely, however, to insist that we must manage these changes in ways that protect not just the business but also the *people* of the kingdom. Change may be necessary. But must it be difficult and destructive? And must the fracture line of change always run between generations?

In the 145th Psalm, David envisions a period of worship in which multiple generations raise a common song in praise to God…an expression of worship that lasts *forever and ever*. Admittedly, David's poem does not address the issue of change and how older and younger generations handle change. It does, however, stress the importance of different generations singing from the same score. It does suggest that only a faith shared by different generations can last forever. And it raises the interesting question of how different generations can be persuaded to sing the same song.

The fact that David's vision involves worship is significant. This "man after God's own heart" introduced more worship "innovations" to Israel than anyone else from Moses to Christ. He initiated the transition from tabernacle to temple. Scholars believe it was David who brought instrumental music (lyres and harps and trumpets) into the worship of Israel. Many of the Psalms were written to be read in worship settings, supplementing the reading of Torah. He added a considerable emphasis on praise to a worship previously dominated by sacrifice and confession.

The fact that the generations of his vision are singing the same song has little to do with an unchanging liturgy and a shared commitment to static religious forms. They are singing together in spite of revolutionary changes in religious expression. They are singing together a song that is, in many and profound ways, new.

And the fact that worship is such a lightning rod between generations in the church today also makes David's vision significant. We struggle with similar changes in religious expression. If we could find a way to handle differences in worship styles, perhaps other changes would be manageable. Can David teach us anything here?

The Grand Chorus

As David begins writing the 145th Psalm, he struggles to find words, to craft phrases that will adequately convey his yearning to exalt and magnify his God. But words seem so transitory, so fleeting. What David wants is a chorus of praise that will last *forever and ever.*

It isn't until the fourth verse of this Psalm that David strikes on a verbal picture robust enough to carry his praise.

One generation will commend your works to another;
    they will tell of your mighty acts.
They will speak of the glorious splendor of your majesty,
    and I will meditate on your wonderful works.
They will tell of the power of your awesome works,
    and I will proclaim your great deeds.
They will celebrate your abundant goodness
    and joyfully sing of your righteousness (vss. 4-7).

David envisions a vast chorus assembled to sing a great song of praise. But, if you listen carefully, you will hear not one chorus but two. On one side is a choir made up of an older generation that stands to sing of God's works and mercies. Facing them is a second choir of younger people—their sons and daughters—who assemble for the same purpose.

This intergenerational chorus is singing *antiphonally* in David's vision. Each side addresses the other in song, while the other listens and then responds. When one chorus praises God, the other sings, "Amen and amen!" When one testifies to God's goodness, the other gives thanks. Each side commends God to the other.

Here is a chorus of praise that can go on forever. The words, though fleeting, are taken up afresh by another choir. One generation dies out—its voice stilled. But a new generation is born to take up the song and continue the praise. One generation commends God to another and trusts the other to sustain the song. In this way, the goodness of God is proclaimed "forever and ever."

There is no hint in this text about which generation does what, which lines are sung by which chorus, which group leads and which follows. David appears to place himself in one of the choruses ("they tell… and I proclaim"), but we cannot know to which he belongs. All we know is that there is dialogue going on. This is no dry monologue where one side lectures while the other takes notes. Each generation encourages the other to sing well and boldly…and is encouraged in turn.

I love this vision. Two generations bound together by a common song. Faith transferred from old to young. Faith reflected back by young to old. Two generations but one faith, one God, one song of praise. But I do have a small question to ask. As these choruses sing, whose language are they using?

The Generation Gap

Dreamy visions are one thing, hard realities another. The truth is that generations don't always communicate with one another as

well as they did in David's psalm. They don't always speak the same
language. They're not always from the same planet.

"I don't understand you!"
                    "That's because you're not listening to me!"
"How many ways do I have to say this?"
                                "Same song, 300th verse!"
"It goes in one ear and out the other!"
                            "I can't tell you anything!"
"Read my lips!"
                    "Your lips are moving but I can't hear you!"
"Man, you don't speak my language!"

Every generation has its own idioms, develops its own tastes,
speaks its own language. My grandfather grew up in the depression,
listened to Big Band music, and wore zoot suits. He would not be
seen outdoors without a hat. My father was shaped by the Second
World War. He enjoyed the Kingston Trio and wore skinny black ties
and white shirts. I came of age during the Vietnam war, singing
Rolling Stones tunes and wearing bell bottomed jeans. My teenaged
daughter watched the Wall fall, listens to Christian rap, and loves to
wear baggy shorts.

Every generation is different. Each expresses itself using a
unique vocabulary. The behavioral dialects that distinguish the generations in America today are just as powerful as the linguistic
dialects that distinguish ethnic groups in Eastern Europe or Africa.

It is not always easy for one generation to understand, much less
appreciate, another generation. That's true of music, fashion, and
values. It's even more true of something as sensitive as faith.

The generation gap has frustrated many an effort to talk about
faith in a meaningful and mutually encouraging way. Evidently, it
caused problems for Joshua and Caleb: they could not find the
words to persuade an older generation that God would be with
them as they went in to conquer the land. It baffled parents during

the period of the Judges: try as they might, they could not interest their children in a passionate relationship with God. Even Jesus spoke of fathers who would not be able to pass on faith to their children, and children who would not be able to bring their parents to faith.

Instead of one generation "commending God" to another—as in the vision of David—too often generations talk past each other, out-shout each other, stop listening to and give up on each other. The dialogue breaks down, faith falters, and people begin to wonder if God is really the God of all generations.

The Battle of the Generations

We find ourselves at such a juncture in many of our churches today. Every one of us wants what David dreamed of. We long to belong to a harmonious, happy, intergenerational chorus. Those who are older want to sing of the glories of God and hear younger voices sing the "Amen." Those who are younger want to shout God's praise and hear their elders say, "Hallelujah!" We would love a dialogue in which each generation is encouraged to sing joyfully and gratefully and boldly.

The problem is that, too often, each generation insists that the song be sung exclusively in its own language. An older generation wants to sing from the hymnal—"Praise God from whom all blessings flow…." A younger generation wants to sing from projection screens—"Knowing you, Jesus, knowing you…." Each generation insists that its song be embraced by the other. What begins as chorus ends in cacophony. The singing on each side gets louder and louder in an attempt to drown out competing melodies. We grow annoyed with each other for messing up the harmony that could exist—if only you would sing my song! We stick our fingers in our ears, to better hear ourselves sing and block out another generation's worship.

But there is no listening. There is no dialogue. There is no antiphony of praise. We stop communicating with each other and with God. We talk past, shout down, sing over the very people we claim to love most.

Why are we at such an impasse today? I suggest we are there because we do not believe our God is the God of *all* generations. He is the God of *my* generation. But not yours.

The Problem of Religious Language

There is an older generation in the church today who apparently believes God is monolinguistic—and can speak only the language in which *they* happen to be fluent.

When that generation gathers to sing, "Night with Ebon Pinion," when it opens and closes all its worship services with a prayer, when it tells its preachers to include fewer stories and more Bible verses, when it serves the Supper *before* the sermon, never *after*—that generation believes God understands and appreciates the language they offer.

When an older generation attends gospel meetings and funds foreign mission efforts and supports children's homes—it believes it is engaging in ministry that God values.

When that generation gathers on Sunday morning, Sunday night, and Wednesday night, when it says "Amen" when expressing agreement and support, when it puts on a coat and tie (or a best dress) to attend worship—that generation is expressing faith in the only language it knows, believing that God hears and understands.

So here gathers one generational choir. All speak the same language. All learned the same ways. All practice the same tradition. And they eagerly invite a younger generation to join them in a chorus of praise. "Only, for the sake of harmony, let's sing *our* songs, let's say *our* prayers, let's honor *our* traditions, let's do things *our* way. If you will just learn my language, we can sing together as we praise God."

But guess what? There's a younger generation in the church today just as convinced God is limited to one language—*their* language.

That generation sings, "I love you, Lord, and I lift my hands...." It appreciates variety in its worship services. It might open worship with a song and close with a responsive reading. There is little that is predictable or set. The preaching of a younger generation is less informational and more motivational. It serves coffee and donuts in the foyer and believes fellowship is as legitimate a reason for gathering as Bible study or devotionals. When this generation does such things, it believes God hears and understands the language it speaks.

This younger generation is less inclined to do gospel meetings or support foreign missions. It is more likely to plan marriage seminars and support a vibrant youth ministry and become involved in community efforts. But it believes that these, also, are ministries that God values.

This generation is not eager to come back on Sunday nights, but loves to spend weekends with brothers and sisters on retreats. On Wednesday nights, it would prefer to gather in small groups in the intimacy of each other's homes. This generation doesn't say "Amen" to express agreement—it breaks into applause. And when it wears shorts and sandals to worship, it means no disrespect—it simply knows that God is looking at the heart, not the manner of dress.

So here sits a *second* generational choir. Like the first, its members also speak a similar language, share similar views and opinions, are comfortable with their own ways. For all their boasting about individuality, the younger generation is just as homogeneous as the older.

And they, just as eagerly and naively, invite the older generation to join them in a chorus of praise. "Only, why don't you guys speak *our* language today. Sing *our* songs, clap with us, do things *our* way. Let's shake things up a little bit so we can joyfully praise our God together!"

The result of each generation demanding its own way is a standoff. An older generation insists *its* language be used by all. A younger generation is just as insistent that *its* language be used. Each generation disparages the language of the other, claiming that God is not nearly so fluent in the language of the other generation as he is in *my* generation's dialect. Me and mine speak the vernacular that God best understands and appreciates.

Instead of a chorus, we have bedlam. Instead of a united song, we have competing chants. Instead of praise, we have problems.

Our Multilingual God

Have we forgotten that we commune with a God who spoke Ugaritic to Abraham, Hebrew to David, Aramaic to Peter, Greek to Timothy, Latin to Augustine, German to Luther, and English to us? Our God has never been limited by the Babel of languages that divide us. He has never been monolinguistic. He hears, understands, and appreciates the speech of the heart, no matter what language is used to express it. He is the God of all languages.

And have we forgotten that we worship a God who can appreciate the Jewish worship of the Jerusalem church, the Gentile worship of the Antioch church, the ignorant worship of some Ephesian Christians (Acts 19:1ff), and the charismatic free-for-all worship of the Corinthians? No one culture has a monopoly on God. He hears, understands, and appreciates the speech of the heart, no matter what culture or customs it is wrapped in. He is the God of all cultures.

How, then, can we imagine we are dealing with a "my generation" God? Our God listens to old and young. He understands the language of both. He listens past our words and our habits and our preferences to hear the heart that beats beneath. And the heart has a language that transcends generation. God is the God of all generations.

A God for All Generations

One generation will commend your works to another;
 they will tell of your mighty acts.

David's vision of a harmonious, intergenerational chorus singing praises to God is still possible in our time. We can find a way to join generations in a dialogue of praise, singing one rousing, soul-thrilling song to God.

But it will not happen by one generation insisting that its own language provide the norm for the church. It will not happen by one generation overpowering or out-shouting another. Praise will not result from a successful struggle for power.

The key is for each generation to acknowledge that it has something to learn from the other, that a portion of each generation's language can be adopted by the other, that a melding of languages can make one common language possible. It will be part old and part young, both traditional and contemporary, a little of the past and a bit of the future.

I have a dream that one day old and young will gather for worship in churches across our country. There, they will array themselves into two great choruses. The old will begin the song, "Praise God from whom all blessings flow..." and the young will sing back the "Amen." The young will then sing out, "I was made to praise you Jesus..." and the old will break into applause.

The old will sing, "Lord we come before thee now, at thy feet we humbly bow..." and the young will kneel down because they know it will encourage the older. Then the young will sing, "With my hands lifted high..." and gnarled, old hands will go up all over the auditorium, not because such a thing is comfortable but because it encourages a new generation of faith.

I dream of a church where one Sunday there is silence during the Supper in respect for the old, while the next Sunday there is singing and testimony in deference to the young. One Sunday, the old endure (even learn to enjoy?) drama because they know how powerfully it speaks to their children, while the next Sunday, the young endure (even learn to appreciate?) sixteenth-century hymns because they know how powerfully such hymns speak to their parents.

I dream of a church where each generation is humble enough to confess it does not yet speak in the tongues of angels. I dream of a church where the old are willing to defer to the young and the young are eager to defer to the old. I dream of a church where many languages can be spoken and appreciated as different people and different generations attempt to join together in praise of God.

If we can become such a church, then the possibility exists for praise that can go on forever. One generation's faith can be taken up afresh by another. As one generation dies out, a new generation is born to take up the song and continue the worship. One generation commends God to another and trusts the other to carry on the song. In this way, the goodness of God is proclaimed "forever and ever." Such a goal is worth the effort and discomfort involved in learning to speak and appreciate another generation's language.[1]

A Concluding Word

Constants and Contingencies

Modern flying machines confront us with a baffling variety of form. There are planes pushed by propellers and jet engines. There are two-seater Cessnas and five hundred passenger 747s and monstrous cargo-carrying transports. There are fixed-wing, variable-wing, and rotary-wing aircraft. Crop-dusters fly at tree-top level, while spy planes soar in the stratosphere and rockets thunder into space.

None of them looks very bird-like. None of them boasts feather-covered flappers. But all of them fly because they take advantage of the same aerodynamic principles that allow birds to glide and dart. There are certain fundamentals to flight—lift, thrust, resistance, control—that cannot be ignored. They are the constants that must govern any bird or machine that ventures into thin air.

It was these "constants" to which the pioneers of flight had to turn in their quest to build a flying machine. They stopped their anatomical studies of bird wings. They put down their magnifying glasses and dissection knives. And they turned to something even more basic. They built wind tunnels. They conducted careful aerodynamic studies. They learned some principles to which even birds submit.

That single act—disconnecting the bird-form from the flight-function—allowed the Wright brothers to achieve flight without having to mimic the manner in which birds did so. They designed a machine to honor aerodynamic principles, though it did not look very bird-like in the end.

What the Wright brothers could not predict (what they could not imagine) was the vast variety of flying forms those principles would permit. It turns out that freedom of form becomes possible within the context of faithfulness to fundamentals. A rocket can provide lift as well as the wing of a plane or the rotating blades of a helicopter. Different forms, same function. Vectored jets of gas function like wing flaps or a tail rotor to provide control. Different means, same end. When you understand *why* things fly, *how* is limited only by those fundamentals and your own ingenuity.

This book has attempted to build a similar wind tunnel for the church. My concern has been to set down some principles for being the people of God—some "constants" for doing kingdom business—that go beyond anatomical sketches of the early church. I want to understand how the winds of time and culture buffet and destabilize us. I want to know why certain church forms worked so well for God's people there and then, but function so poorly here and now. I am concerned about the spiritual vertigo induced by tiny things…and the seeming lack of a spiritual compass to keep us moving toward things that matter.

Basic to this effort has been a willingness to disconnect form from function and to inquire whether there are principles for being the church that are more basic than the methods and means used by churches two thousand years removed. I've put down my paring knife. I'm looking for something that can never be seen with a magnifying glass.

I believe those principles are there, lying beneath the particular practices of Abraham and Moses and Paul, the church of

Corinth and the church of Jerusalem. The practices are recorded to instruct us, not to enslave us. They point beyond themselves to some deeper realities about God's people and God's work.

The time has come for those of us in the Churches of Christ to go back to school and take flying lessons all over again. It is time for us to become reacquainted with the fundamentals that provided lift and thrust and control for the church of the first-century. It is time, past time, for us to cease obsessing about the color of the fuselage and the seating arrangements in the cabin... to focus instead on that which is fundamental and essential for getting our churches off the ground.

When we understand *why* the church exists and *what* God has called us to do, we may well discover a freedom regarding form that strengthens, rather than undermines, our ability to be a faithful church. We may discover that the greatest challenge to a restoration people is to fly *with* the New Testament church, to identify and restore that part of God's ancient business and God's ancient people that is truly fundamental. And we may discover that such a commitment will require an inventiveness, a creativity of form, that necessarily makes us look different from our ancient counterpart.

Appendix

The Otter Creek Family of Faith

I am about to do something dangerous. I am about to take the principles of this book, pour them into the setting of a particular church, and then attempt to describe what that looks like. To share what is happening at the church for which I preach, to discuss our failures and victories as we try to be "a church that flies," to admit some of the roadblocks and conflicts along the way, requires saying more about Otter Creek than is safe. It requires me to walk a very fine and dangerous line.

On the one hand, you (the reader) may find it valuable to view these principles in a specific setting—to think about how the ideas of this book might impact the teaching, programming, decision-making, and leadership of a particular congregation.

On the other hand, to hold up any church as an example of a congregation pursuing the principles of this book poses real problems:

1. *It could communicate arrogance*—that we think ourselves to be the only or the best example of a Church of Christ attempting to be shaped by function rather than form. That is not the case.

2. *It could communicate separation*—that, somehow, we are attempting to distance ourselves from our movement. Again, that is not the case. Our desire is to remain firmly within the Restoration Heritage even as we attempt to be the church God is calling us to be. We want to make this journey arm-in-arm with our movement, not separate and apart from it.

3. *It could portray an unrealistic picture*—suggesting there is greater unity, less failure, fewer debates, and more victories than is actually the case. We are not finding this process easy at Otter Creek. We have made and will make more than our share of mistakes. Our membership is composed of strong-willed, heavily-invested, deeply-spiritual people who shout and cry

and question at every move along the way. If the description below suggests a church moving in lock-step toward a particular destination, that is a convenient fiction adopted for the sake of space.

4. *It could tie these principles to the fate of a particular church.* Perhaps this is the greatest danger of all. Ultimately, Otter Creek may fail to be a church that knows its business and pursues it. But does that mean the principles are wrong? Does the failure of one church mean that others should give up the attempt? Whether we succeed or fail (or—better—whatever the mix of success and failure we must live with), the functions of God's people cannot be held hostage by the inability of a particular group of Christians to live up to them.

A Little History and Orientation

Located in south Nashville, the Otter Creek Church was founded in 1929. The first building, erected in 1930, was made from the timber, doors, and windows of David Lipscomb's dismantled home. In 1950, the church moved to it's present site and built the auditorium and classroom wing that are the cornerstone of our current facility.

But bricks and mortar are not the real story at Otter Creek. This church has always had a heart for serving its community and ministering to those in need. In the 1950's, responding to a growing number of orphans and children up for adoption, Otter Creek was instrumental in founding Agape—a family oriented ministry directly responsible for spawning 15 other agencies that help with adoption, foster care and family counseling. In the '60s, Otter Creek (in particular, Ruth Rucker) started a preschool—teaching Christian principles to neighborhood children. That ministry now reaches hundreds of children each year and has become widely known and respected in Nashville. This church has been drawn to mission works in some of the neediest areas of the world, including Korea (during the '60s and '70s—when we helped found not only churches but educational institutions), and South America (during the '80s and '90s—when we coupled missionary activity with medical missions). Recently, the church built a $750,000 day care center in downtown Nashville to care for poor children while their mothers are at work.

Our current attendance runs above 900 people on Sunday mornings. Members are predominantly Church of Christ in background (though people from all sorts of religious background are worshipping with us). We are composed of doctors and lawyers, educators and entrepreneurs, musicians and artists, nurses and mechanics. As a whole, our members are well educated, upper middle class, strong in personality and opinions, and deeply concerned about spiritual matters. Leading such a group is like herding cats. They won't be driven, but they can be drawn.

Perhaps the most important thing for you to know about Otter Creek is this: we are sewn together by a common sense of our own sinfulness and failure, of God's mercy and rich grace, of Christ's transforming power in our lives personally, and of our need for each other.

There is much more that could be said about Otter Creek. (You can check out our web site—www.ottercreek.org—for more information.) But perhaps this will be enough orientation for present purposes.

My Ministry at Otter Creek

I came to Otter Creek in the summer of 1998. Nashville was new for me. Most of my ministry has been outside the "Bible Belt." To be thrown into a culture so saturated not just with religion but with such a surplus of Church of Christ heritage came as a shock (in the best and worst sense of that word).

Before accepting the work at Otter Creek, I wanted the elders to know that I was committed to a particular vision of how the church should work. I came not so much with an agenda as a sense of mission… an understanding of what we should be about as a church.

This book had been banging around in me for several years. I already had the first half written. The Westside Church in Portland, Oregon, was the Petrie dish in which these ideas developed and were cultivated. Ron Stump, my cohort in that work, helped me stir and test and implement the brew. There was enough invested in these ideas, I had no interest in moving to a church that would not tolerate some coloring outside the lines.

I photocopied the parts of the manuscript that were finished (how did Paul ever make it without a laptop and Xerox?) and asked the elders at Otter Creek to read it. I wanted everything on the table before I came.

Our next meeting amazed me. They assured me that what I had written was essentially what Otter Creek had been trying to do for years. They showed me planning documents and written pieces and mission statements that addressed most of the functions I had outlined as essential "Kingdom business." They wanted me to know that the things I believed to be important about "doing church" were values they shared. Their desire to focus on those functions was as strong as mine. They also saw the danger of obsessing over forms, of letting the "how" overwhelm the "what" and "why." They wanted Otter Creek to be a church where function came first.

On that basis, I agreed to move to Nashville, feeling that God had led me to a group of elders and a family of faith who shared my desire to build a church that would put first things first.

Building a Mission Statement

Until you can say—specifically, concretely—what you are trying to do, it is impossible to move ahead purposefully or to communicate where you want to go. As Charlie Brown says, "Unless you know where you're going, how will you know when you get there?" Otter Creek had the momentum of her heritage, history, and the personalities making up her membership. But in order to move forward towards a goal, rather than simply be carried forward by the momentum of our past, we all felt it was necessary to state clearly where we wanted to go. That meant crafting a mission statement that covered the kingdom business I believed to be essential while also incorporating the language and ideals that were already basic to Otter Creek. The statement had to be a marriage of core beliefs, Otter Creek themes, and our hopes for the future.

The elders, ministry coordinators (our deacons), and ministry staff met to talk through the seven functions of the church. We talked about them during regular meetings. We called special meetings to explore them further. We went on retreats. We opened our Bibles to see the people of God at work in various ways throughout history. We prayed that God would fill us with a burning desire, a holy ambition, to become a church that was dedicated to His business—balanced in our commitments, wise in our methods, and loving in our pursuit of His agenda.

I learned that "incarnation" had been an important theme at Otter Creek—the church becoming Christ's presence for the community and the world. I learned that the working of the Spirit and the centrality of grace were themes which had deep roots in the history of this church. All these notions were also central to my preaching and theology. I felt another confirmation of God's guidance—bringing me together with a church where these themes were taken seriously.

Over the course of these meetings and discussions, as we sought God's leading and will, a consensus began to build about what a mission statement should include. Here is what one of my elders calls the "Luby's

Cafeteria" description of Otter Creek—what you say to someone who asks about Otter Creek when you're standing in line at a restaurant and you have 20 seconds to respond:

> *The Otter Creek Church is a Christ-centered, Spirit-powered, grace-motivated family of believers. Our mission is to:*
>> *Reach up through worship and holy living*
>> *Reach in by building community and Christ-like lives*
>> *Reach out through service, witness, and Christian influence.*
> *God is changing the world through us as we become Christ's presence in this place.*

It is a statement in three segments:

1. We wanted our statement to include the basic power sources of our church's life. So the first sentence identifies Christ, the Spirit, and grace as the driving forces of Otter Creek. Jesus leads and we follow. We do so not by our own strength or competence but by the power of the Spirit who dwells in us. And we do what we do out of gratitude and thanksgiving for what God has done for us. While we owe a great debt to our heritge, we are led by our understanding of Christ's will, not the traditions of our movement. The Spirit of God, dwelling in us and speaking through the written Word, teaches, convicts, and changes us. Though sometimes guilt or obligation or a sense of duty will motivate our individual actions, as a church we want to live principally out of gratitude.

2. It is easy to see how the seven functions weave their way through the middle segment of this statement: worship, holiness, community, maturing (building Christ-like lives), service, witness, and Christian influence. We thought it appropriate to group these functions into three categories—categories that define the audiences we feel called to serve. The church exists for God, and so we reach up through worship and holiness. The church exists for the world, and so we serve needs and witness to the cross and act as salt. And the church also exists for itself, reaching in to build intimacy and people who look like Jesus.

Notice that our mission addresses function. It stresses what we are called to do, not how we intend to do it. It implies that our identity is rooted in a common source of power that is used to accomplish a valued set of goals. Our identity as a church is not centered on the forms we use or the particular methods we employ but on the essential business we hope to accomplish.

3. The final segment addresses our ambitions. We desire to become Christ's presence in the world (the incarnation theme). We want to make ourselves available to God, for His work and purposes. And we intend to change the world as a result. We are about no little business, conducted in a corner, for minimal gains. We do not think it is immodest to believe that Christ's presence and God's power at work in us will have world-changing impact. We hope it does and expect that it will.

Communicating the Mission Statement

As we came closer to a consensus on a mission statement, I began to teach a combined adult class, and to introduce ideas about the seven functions, the relationship between form and function, and how a church recovers a sense of mission for God. Our members had a chance to wrestle with these ideas. And I had a chance to hear their questions and suggestions.

We grappled with the notion that the longer we are about the business of faith (and the more complicated faith becomes, the greater the accumulation of tradition and habit), the more difficult it becomes to identify what is central. We confessed a tendency to make the trivial important and demote the important to the status of the trivial. We talked about change, when it was appropriate, when it was necessary.

I also began a short sermon series (called—what else?—"A Church that Flies"), including sermons on: "Getting about God's Business," "The Big Rocks Go in First," "Power for Living," and "Purpose and Passion."

As the class and sermon series were winding down, we designed a graphic that could be used in communicating our mission statement and building familiarity with it. Over a photo of our people gathered in worship, we screened our mission statement. Kinkos printed these out in large 36" x 24" posters that were hung in each of our teen and adult classrooms. We digitized this image and project it on overhead screens before and after worship services. About once a month, I weave the statement into a sermon and have the congregation say it together. We print the statement every week on the masthead of our bulletin. We go over it with new members. It hangs in the conference room where our elders meet so they can refer to it and be reminded of what we are about.

Most of our members haven't memorized this statement yet, but they know what it is. They don't understand everything about it, but they grasp that it defines the core of our life together. Not everyone has bought into it, but they recognize how important it is to our leadership and our future.

Shaping the Church by the Mission Statement

If the church is, in fact, "commissioned," if it has a particular work to do in this world, you would expect that mission to shape the teaching and programming of the congregation. At Otter Creek, the next few years have been planned with our Mission Statement very much in mind.

Creating an Environment for a Functional Church

Just as many songs are written around a chorus that repeats throughout the song, so the church has to be shaped around certain themes that come up often and repeatedly. Finding those core themes and sounding them effectively is one of the greatest challenges for preachers and church leaders.

Mine are reflected in Otter Creek's Mission Statement. They have to do with who Jesus is and where he would lead us, how the Spirit works in and empowers us, the importance of grace to living the Christian life. They have to do with being a church that incarnates Christ, having God-sized ambitions, keeping our focus on what is important.

Take any five-year preaching cycle, and you will find my preaching coming back to these ideas with regularity. They create a necessary environment for talking about the church's mission and identity. In order to talk about our work, we have to understand our power source. Before we can understand our mission, we need a clear sense of direction and motivation.

So I talk a lot about the cross and resurrection. I sprinkle studies of the gospels among other preaching plans. We'll do seminars on the Holy Spirit and retreats on how Otter Creek can be the aroma of Christ. We'll keep coming back to these themes in various ways and in regular cycles. These are the primary colors we work with at Otter Creek. Every other shade and hue is based on them.

Building a Church Around these Functions

Early on, I asked my elders to evaluate Otter Creek using the seven functions. Where were we strong and where weak?

They ranked Otter Creek's strengths and weaknesses in the following way (from greatest strength to greatest weakness):

1. Worship—We have a long history of vibrant worship leaders and worship services. New members see this as one of our greatest strengths.

2. Community—There is a strong sense of family at Otter Creek. Our people love each other. We have structured the church to encourage intimacy (through small groups, our Sunday School structure, etc.)

3. Service—We have a history here as well. However, inducting newer members into that service mind-set and passing on an ethic of service to the future is a concern.

4. Maturity—We have many people who demonstrate Christ-like lives and attitudes. However, we also have many who, by reason of time, should be mature but aren't. And we are being flooded by young people who need our help growing up into Christ.

5. Witness—Otter Creek has always wanted a vital witness to the lost, but we have rarely found our stride. Good has been accomplished through the missionaries we support. But reaching our local community has been an ongoing challenge for us.

6. Holiness—Though we encourage holy living, we do so mostly by talking about moral living. Even then, we are tainted by the immorality of our culture. But notions like the Disciplines, calling, giftedness, consecration are too rarely discussed and understood.

7. Influence—The idea that we should deliberately act as salt and light, that we should take an active role in shaping our community and tuning its sensibilities has never been one of our strengths. We need to learn more about what this means and how this can be accomplished.

On the basis of their evaluation, we set out a calendar for the next few years, devoting time and attention in the church's life to addressing these matters.

Currently (as I write), we are focusing on Maturity. Much of the preaching and programming of the church centers on growing up in Christ. I am preaching on the Beatitudes (which I see as an instruction manual for becoming the person Jesus wants us to be); on maturity themes like put off/put on, the new man, the imitation of Christ; on the fruits of the Spirit. We will be reading through the Bible as a congregation. We are starting a mentoring program where those who are older can take an active role in encouraging growth in younger Christians. We will give our members an opportunity to assess their own level of maturity—and visit with an elder to discuss how the church can help them grow up in "fullness."

In coming years, we will carve out seasons where we emphasize the other "functions" of God's people. Our preaching and programming will center on "witness" or "holiness" or one of the other core functions for an extended period of time. We'll grapple with what these things look like and how we can nurture them individually and as a church. The agenda of the church is essentially shaped by our desire to address these seven functions and make them priorities in the life of the Otter Creek family.

And what happens when we work through all seven? We start over again. We dig deeper. We reaffirm our commitment to God's business and press even harder toward the goal for which we have been called. This is the business of Otter Creek. If we get this right, we are convinced we can't go far wrong. And we refuse to be distracted from this business by the tiny things Satan throws up to blind and busy us.

Which is one of the greatest advantages of focusing a church on what matters. No church is safe from being tyrannized by tiny things. Any church can have its agenda hijacked by issues which seem so urgent but, in the end, lack any real importance. Only those churches that deliberately, stubbornly, keep their focus on the core can avoid getting sidetracked by the peripheral.

Dealing with Conflict

Of course, we are as vulnerable to a hijacking of purpose as anyone. Even when a leadership keeps its focus on things that matter, there are many others whose focus is elsewhere. Because we love and honor these people, we feel responsible to spend time on issues we would rather avoid. Let me give one example.

Like many Churches of Christ, worship style is a lightening rod for conflict at Otter Creek. We have a Praise Team and project songs on screens and (at times) dispense with a traditional invitation. We use clips from movies and dramatic sketches and special music. The "order of worship" varies greatly from week to week.

As you can imagine, this is a source of some conflict at Otter Creek. The elders believe that God wants us to be a worshipping people. They further believe that helping people to worship, leading them into the throne room of God, is a constant challenge that will not be met by strict adherence to a traditional worship formula. So they encourage the staff to "use every relevant means of worship and praise" to usher our congregation into God's presence.

This emphasis on function, however, brings us into conflict with some of our own members who have habituated to certain forms. We have members who don't like the Praise Team. They don't appreciate more contemporary songs. They don't want singing during the Lord's Supper. They want a formal invitation (along with a homily on baptism) every week.

They hate drama and video clips. They want shape notes to accompany the words to songs.

How do we deal with these concerns?

We defer when we can. At present, for example, we do not sing during the Supper to accommodate the sensibilities of members who are "offended" by this practice. When deferring can help some and does not harm others, we believe this is an appropriate and godly course of action.

Many times, however, we find ourselves in a position where deferring to one set of sensibilities causes us to trample over the sensibilities of others. You may not like a Praise Team, but others are edified and moved to worship by their ministry. I may not like contemporary songs, but our college students sing them with heart-felt fervor. Some may want a formal invitation, but for others the invitation has lost all meaning and power to compel.

In such circumstances, loving compromise is the appropriate course. At Otter Creek, we use a Praise Team but (often) have them sitting on the first row rather than standing before the congregation. Brandon Scott Thomas (our worship leader) makes a conscious effort to mix old and new music into our worship—so that every week we sing some ancient hymns and some modern songs of praise. Though we use video and drama on occasion, we do not do so every week.

To be truthful, compromises of this sort do not satisfy everyone. Some people will insist that their opinions or convictions be honored—in spite of and over the needs of others. Our elders refuse to show such preference or partiality. They will offer compromise. But, where that does not suffice, they are not afraid to offer the door.

Both deference and compromise, however, are offered in a context. That context is the insistence that people continue to grow and mature in Christ. Someone who believes it is sinful to sing during the Supper is (in our humble opinion) betraying a lack of spiritual discernment and maturity. He or she is making a judgment where God has not. We may defer to such a conviction for a time. But we do so expecting that person to grow and develop in his or her understanding of God's will. We may compromise about where the Praise Team stands (or sits) because we honor people who are uncomfortable with their standing before the congregation. But we do so in full expectation that such a person will come to understand that their discomfort is not the yardstick by which God measures a church's faithfulness.

Note, however, that what our elders defer to or compromise on today, they may refuse to show deference to or compromise on a year from now. For the expectation is that God's people should be growing up into full understanding. Making minor things major, putting emphasis where God has not, and—most of all—letting forms get in the way of functions, are symptoms of immaturity and spiritual blindness. Sometimes a church can defer to that. Often, we are patient with that. But the time does come when a congregation can no longer be held hostage to one person's stubborn and out-of-all-proportion opinion. That person should be challenged to grow up. If he or she refuses, the problem runs far deeper than an addiction to shape notes and three point sermons.

All of which highlights the responsibility of church leaders to lead. The agenda for any church will be set either by those who champion the tiny or those who keep the church focused on its primary work. Church leaders must keep us focused on the big picture.

Do they listen to people who can't see the forest for the trees? Yes. But not to the detriment of the forest. They don't spend three quarters of a meeting wrestling with things that, in the end, don't matter, while never quite getting around to essential business.

And they have a responsibility to educate, to encourage and exhort, the people they listen to. It's amazing how many church members are quite willing to voice their opinions to elders and quite reticent to listen and learn from them. True leaders recognize that voiced opinions are opportunities for teaching, not commands which must be obeyed.

Our hope is that by focusing on mission, by keeping first things first, by attending to "weightier matters," we can keep the tiny in its place and do the essential business God has called us to do.

If we can be a church characterized by authentic worship, genuine holiness, loving community, Christ-like maturity, selfless service, bold witness and tangible influence—that will be enough for me. How we do those things, who we please or displease along the way, what means and methods we employ are of lesser importance. What matters most is that we focus on things that matter and accomplish the business God has called his people to do.

Notes

Chapter 1: Ornithopterists and Their Spiritual Cousins

[1]There is, of course, a much longer history of such attempts in other religious movements through history. The Puritans were also enamored with a restoration ideal. See T. D. Bozeman, *To Live Ancient Lives: The Primitivist Dimension in Puritanism* (University of North Carolina Press, 1988).

Chapter 2: On a Mission from God

[1]Oliver Sacks, *The Man Who Mistook His Wife for a Hat* (Touchstone Books, 1998).

[2]See Richard Hughes and Leonard Allen, *Illusions of Innocence: Protestant Primitivism in America, 1630-1875* (University of Chicago Press, 1988), 170ff. "[Alexander Campbell] proclaimed in the Christian Baptist in 1825 that 'just in so far as the ancient order of things, or the religion of the New Testament, is restored, just so far has the Millennium commenced.'"

Chapter 3: The Christ-Shaped Church

[1]Rubel Shelly and Randall Harris, *The Second Incarnation* (Howard Publishing, 1992), 62. This book treats at length an idea I can only spend a single chapter on.

[2]Ibid., 53-54.

[3]This was as true for Israel as for the church. Many Mosaic commands (e.g., the Sabbath, holiness, treatment of the fatherless and widows) were rooted in aspects of God's behavior and character. Israel was to evidence these traits because they were characteristic of God. They were, in some sense, to incarnate Yahweh by conducting themselves in a manner reflective of His personality.

But there was something distinctly Christological as well about the law of Moses. The Hebrew writer makes clear that God intended the Jewish cultus to incarnate Jesus at every level. "[The] sanctuary...is a copy and shadow of what is in heaven" (Heb. 8:5). "The law is only a shadow of the good things that are coming—not the realities themselves" (Heb. 10:1). Thus the priesthood, the sacrifices, the curtain and the Holy of Holies—all prefigured the work of Jesus. They incarnated the Son even before he took on a physical body.

[4]Ibid., 28-29.

[5]See Mark 1:38; 2:17; 10:45; John 6:38; 9:39; 10:10; 12:46-47; 18:37.

Chapter 4: Form and Function: A Distinction that Matters

[1]Robert Pirsig, *Zen and the Art of Motorcycle Maintenance: An Inquiry into Values* (Bantam Books, 1984).

²Some, no doubt, will counter that the prophets do not advocate getting rid of the temple or sacrifice or circumcision, but only that (in addition to these forms) Israel pay attention to holy living, etc. They are not saying that forms are dispensable, but that functions come first. There is certainly truth to that point. However, as we will see in later chapters, during times when certain forms were impossible (e.g., after the destruction of the temple), Israel was still called to function as God's people. In reality, circumstances did "get rid" of the temple and the sacrifices—yet Israel could still function as a holy, worshipping, God-centered community.

Chapter 5: The Seven Functions of God's People
¹Stephen Covey, Roger Merrill, and Rebecca Merrill, *First Things First* (Simon & Schuster, 1994), 88-89.

²It is instructive to observe how others have tried to enumerate the basic functions of the church.

a. Howard Snyder speaks of the "necessary functions of worship, community, leadership, nurture and witness" [*The Community of the King* (Intervarsity Press, 1977), 143].

b. Donald Bloesch [in *Wellsprings of Renewal* (Intervarsity Press, 1977), 108] lists seven marks of "a biblically based community or brotherhood in the world today: 1) it should be genuinely evangelical, committed to the gospel and drawing its principle inspiration from the Bible; 2) it should be a small-scale model of the Church, thus visibly demonstrating the reality of the Christian community; 3) it should be an agent of reconciliation between the churches, being in the proper sense catholic as well as evangelical; 4) it should be outreaching, with an evangelistic missionary fervor; 5) it will be in conflict with the principal values and spirit of surrounding culture, thus demonstrating the line between the Church and the world; 6) it should be an eschatological sign of the coming kingdom of God by its radical witness to the Lordship of Christ; and 7) it should give time to study and instruction as well as prayer and proclamation."

c. Rick Warren, in his recent book *The Purpose Driven Church: Growth without Compromising your Message and Mission* (Zondervan, 1995), 103-107, bases the purposes (or functions) of the church on Mt. 22:37-40 and Mt. 28:19-20. He sees five: worship, ministry, evangelism, fellowship, and discipleship.

d. Rubel Shelly and Randall Harris (in *Second Incarnation*) also address the essential functions of the church—the "theological principles" that the church is called upon to embody. They devote chapters to the church as incarnation, community, worship, mission, and evangelism.

Other examples could be listed. What is interesting is that a wide spectrum of people have seen a core of functions at the heart of being God's people. While there are certainly differences in their lists, the similarities are striking.

³For example: Sinai, the occupation of Canaan, the capture of Jerusalem, the

building of the temple, the re-building of the temple under Ezra and the walls of Jerusalem under Nehemiah.

[4]Exodus, Deuteronomy, Job, Psalms.

[5]See Acts 2:46; 5:12; 20:8; 24:14; Rom. 16:5; 1 Cor. 5:4; 11:17-18; 16:9; Heb. 10:25.

[6]Shelly and Harris, in *Second Incarnation*, have an excellent discussion of worship (see pp. 113ff). I am especially indebted to their debunking of two myths that plague our troubled relationship with the subject of worship: the all-of-life-is-worship notion (frequently used to downplay the importance of corporate worship) and the idea that assembled worship is primarily for the purpose of edification (an insidious thought that undermines the very heart of worship).

[7]See Rom. 12:13, 16; Gal. 5:13; Eph. 4:32; Col. 3:13; 1 Thess. 5:11 and many other references.

[8]See Eph. 2:19-22; 4:25; 1 Cor. 12:12ff.

[9]See the interesting article by John E. Boswell, "Expositio and Oblatio: The Abandonment of Children and the Ancient and Medieval Family," *American Historical Review* 89 (February 1984) 10-33.

Chapter 6: Building a Functional Church

[1]If even visitors came to this conclusion as a result of attending Christian worship, how much more the members themselves!

[2]By either logic or caprice, we have weeded out other "acts" that (though also connected to New Testament worship) are not seen to be binding or part of the pattern—tongues, prophecy, testimony, confession, healing, love feasts, and church discipline, to name a few.

[3]James B. Torrance, *Worship, Community, and the Triune God of Grace* (InterVarsity Press, 1996), 15-16.

[4]One reason for this involves the ever-changing conditions and circumstances in which Christians must live—changes a list could never keep up with. Contrary to popular opinion, Christian ethic has always been more complicated than keeping a few commands here, observing a few prohibitions there. Morality—even Christian morality—is "situational" to the extent that the high calling of Christ contacts different cultures and different challenges.

You can see this struggle to define a Christian ethic in the New Testament itself. Was it right for Christians to eat meat sacrificed to idols? Yes and no, depending on conscience and companions. What did modesty require in Jerusalem, and how did that differ from standards of modesty in Corinth? When should marriage be "honored by all" and when was it "good for a man not to marry"? Under what circumstances was circumcision advised or prohibited? Why was it wrong to be angry in certain situations, while other situations demanded righteous anger? How could a Christian be "all things to all men" and still hold true to his conscience and convictions? One list could never address such complexities. Only a thinking disciple, committed to holy living, could struggle with these issues adequately.

[5]See Eph. 5:1; Phil. 1:27; 2:15; Col. 3:1-2.

[6]See Rom. 8:1-17; 6:15-23; Phil. 3:7-11.

[7]I'm thinking of prohibitions against make-up, movies, card-playing, "mixed bathing," wine, certain hair and dress styles, and like matters.

[8]See Chapter Seven, "The Real Thing," in my book *Walk This Way* (NavPress, 1999), for a deeper discussion of honesty in the family of faith and the dangers of that little word "fine."

[9]See 2 Pet. 3:18; 1 Tim. 4:13; 2 Tim. 3:15-16; Eph. 2:19-20; 4:11-13; Acts 2:42; 1 Tim. 5:17.

[10]See 1 Thess. 1:5b-6a; 1 Cor. 4:15-16; 11:1; Phil. 3:17; 4:9; 2 Thess. 3:9.

[11]See Acts 9:36-39; 11:27-30; Rom. 15:26; 2 Cor. 8:1ff; Jas. 1:27.

[12]As Paul did on numerous occasions—see Acts 22:1ff; 26:9ff; Gal. 1:13ff; 1 Tim. 1:12ff.

[13]See Lk. 24:46-48; Acts 1:8; 2:32; 3:15; 5:32; 10:39-14; Jn. 15:27; 1 Jn. 1:2.

[14]This charge is powerfully corroborated by Bill Love in his book, *The Core Gospel* (ACU Press, 1992). See especially pp. 114-115, 243-258. Love quotes this telling line from F. W. Mattox: "We took for granted that the denominations had saturated society with the teaching of faith and grace and the atonement, and we went about straightening out their misunderstanding of the place, action and order of faith, repentance and baptism in obtaining church membership."

[15] See several devastating quotes in Richard Hughes' book, *Reviving the Ancient Faith: The Story of Churches of Christ in America* (Eerdmans, 1996), esp. chapter 12.

Chapter 7: Form Against Function

[1]Bruce Felton and Mark Fowler, *The Best, Worst and Most Unusual: Noteworthy Achievements, Events, Feats and Blunders of Every Conceivable Kind* (Galahad Books, 1994), 208-209. *Encyclopaedia Britannica*, 1996, "Bell."

[2]The Jubilee is never mentioned outside the Pentateuch, and only once outside the book of Leviticus (although Jubilee language and imagery figures significantly in the Gospels.)

[3]Centuries later, Paul recognized this fact, arguing that covenant (i.e., "righteousness through faith") came before and takes precedence over the physical form of circumcision.

> We have been saying that Abraham's faith was credited to him as right-
> eousness. Under what circumstances was it credited? Was it after he was
> circumcised, or before? It was not after, but before! And he received the
> sign of circumcision, a seal of the righteousness that he had by faith
> while he was still uncircumcised. So then, he is the father of all who
> believe but have not been circumcised, in order that righteousness might
> be credited to them. And he is also the father of the circumcised who
> not only are circumcised but who also walk in the footsteps of the faith
> that our father Abraham had before he was circumcised. (Rom. 4:9-12)

The fact that Yahweh was willing to make covenants with uncircumcised people (an inclination that led ultimately to his inclusion of the Gentiles in the church) plainly indicates that what was of first importance to God was the making and keeping of covenants (a "circumcision of the heart"). Where the form of circumcision supported the function of covenant, well and good. But covenant came first in God's economy, not circumcision.

[4]Paul understood this not only as a perversion of the gospel of Jesus but of the meaning of circumcision itself. Circumcision was given by God as a sign of a covenant that was entered through faith. That it should now be used to prevent covenant with God for people who had confessed faith in Jesus and wanted relationship with Yahweh turned this form on its ear. In Paul's mind, this was a case of the tail wagging the dog—form dominating function rather than serving it. This, Paul would not allow. "Neither circumcision nor uncircumcision means anything; what counts is a new creation" (Gal. 6:15).

[5]The Hebrew writer seems convinced that there was nothing magical or redemptive in the animal sacrifices of the Jews. In his thinking, whatever the sacrifices may have signified for the Jewish people, to God the sacrifices were a stop-gap, an education tool, a symbol pointing to the ultimate (and effective) sacrifice of Jesus.

> The law is only a shadow of the good things that are coming—not the realities themselves. For this reason it can never, by the same sacrifices repeated endlessly year after year, make perfect those who draw near to worship. If it could, would they not have stopped being offered? For the worshipers would have been cleansed once for all, and would no longer have felt guilty for their sins. But those sacrifices are an annual reminder of sins, because it is impossible for the blood of bulls and goats to take away sins.

[6]It took the destruction of Jerusalem and Babylonian captivity to break this notion. How could Israel function in the absence of the altar and the priesthood? 'Quite well' was the answer. By returning to ideals such as personal holiness and consecration (one of the themes of the exilic literature—see Esther, Daniel, Ezra, and Nehemiah), Israel discovered that God would hear her prayers and consider her needs apart from the temple cultus.

[7]Interestingly, Jesus makes this clear in his teaching on the Sabbath. As he points out, priests (who through hard work "desecrate" the day) are, in fact, innocent—they honor the day because their work is an act of submission to God. His own behavior on the Sabbath indicates that one could be quite busy and still honor the intent of the day—to demonstrate submission to the Lord of the Sabbath.

[8]Harry Emerson Fosdick, *The Man from Nazareth as His Contemporaries Saw Him* (Harper and Brothers, 1949), 76.

[9]Dietrich Bonhoeffer, *The Cost of Discipleship* (MacMillan, 1967), 34.

Chapter 8: The Tyranny of the Tiny

[1]Edward Rutherford, *Russka* (Ivy Books, 1991), 409-410.

[2]Jesus uses "blind" five times in this chapter to refer to the Pharisees. "Hypocrites" occurs six times.

Chapter 9: A Life Span for Forms

[1]G. B. Caird, *The Language and Imagery of the Bible* (Westminster Press, 1980), 66.

[2]One of my reviewers made a comment worth repeating. "Cultures (other than the kingdom) may be alive, but are not living in the same sense as the gospel. The gospel always expresses itself culturally, but always challenges and critiques. Effectiveness and culturally appropriate, in my opinion, are often tone-deaf to the distinctive notes of the gospel. They are the sergeant-at-arms for the interests of consumerism." Good point. Sometimes culturally appropriate must mean confrontive or counter-cultural. Thanks Mark.

[3]Ibid., 84.

[4]Shelley and Harris, *Second Incarnation*, 211.

[5]Snyder, *Community of the King*, 168.

Chapter 10: Change and Time

[1]The word "tabernacle" appears 93 times in the NIV in Exodus through Numbers. "Tent of Meeting" occurs 133 times. In contrast, sacrifice(s) was mentioned 79 times, the Sabbath day 31 times, and circumcision only 4 times.

[2]Which has led us, incidentally, to a paradoxical definition of faithfulness. Faithfulness between dispensations requires the acceptance of every change initiated by the new lawgiver; faithfulness within a particular dispensation requires the rejection of every change not explicitly demanded by the lawgiver.

[3] The sin of Nadab and Abihu may have nothing to do with "innovations" or some departure from specifically commanded procedures. Rather, the text (Leviticus 10) suggests that the sin involved here was treating God and their important duties casually, carelessly. They were irreverent and disrespectful, prompting God to insist, "I will be honored!" In fact, the narrative may even indicate that Nadab and Abihu were drunk as they attended to their priestly duties (see v. 8). The first thing God tells their father Aaron is, "You and your sons are not to drink wine or other fermented drink whenever you go into the Tent of Meeting, or you will die." The "strange fire" mentioned in this incident may well refer to insolence rather than innovation.

Chapter 12: A God for All Generations

[1]This chapter is based on a keynote address delivered at the York College Lectureship, October, 1997.

Study Guide

by Doug Sanders & Tim Woodroof

Introduction

This guide is designed to be used in a small group setting—among friends, in a class, or with a church's leadership. It is specifically intended to encourage discussion, research into the Scriptures, and thoughtful analysis of your congregation's practices, principles and "sacred cows." Take it for what it is—a practical application and extension of certain principles that appear in the preceding pages.

The value of this guide will depend on:

1. Prayer—bathe your discussions in prayer.
2. Leadership—someone to start discussion and keep it on track.
3. Familiarity of participants with *A Church that Flies*—each participant needs his or her own copy and should read it.

Discussion Question/Statements/Application

The studies below do not follow the book in any strict order. The point is to learn and apply principles, not review the book. Notice:

1. Each study begins with suggested readings (both from the book and from Scripture). Read these before coming to the group.

2. An overview sets the tone for the discussion to follow. The group leader might want to read the overview aloud and comment.

3. A series of questions, exercises, or statements are listed.

4. The format of this guide is sequential—each page is intended to build on the previous exercise.

5. Much of this guide is informed by the experiences we've had at the Otter Creek Church in Nashville. At the end of this guide, we offer several resources if you're interested, if you want to dig deeper or widen this discussion to your whole church.

Study #1
A COMMISSIONED PEOPLE

Readings:
ACTF pages 1-32, 191-201
1 Cor 12:12-31; Eph 4:1-16; 5:23-33; Col 1:15-24

Overview

As the church, we are called "the body of Christ." If we take that seriously, then the church is meant to be the incarnate Christ—the hands and feet, the heart and mind of Jesus. To put it another way, we have been called to continue Christ's mission—reaching up to the Father, reaching in to build vibrant communities of faith, and reaching out to the lost. What a commission!

Discussion Question/Statements/Application

1. Identify and discuss the "I have come" statements of Jesus— those statements that define his purpose and mission on earth. (Examples from Matthew—5:17; 9:13; 10:34; 20:28.)

2. Is it reasonable to think that, if Christ were to appear on earth today, his ministry would look exactly like it did in the New Testament? In what way would Jesus' work remain the same? In what ways would it differ to match these times and this culture?

3. The gospels tell us how Jesus lived and practiced the principles he valued. The rest of the New Testament shows us how first

2

century Christians applied and lived his teachings. But the pattern is always Jesus, not particular applications by particular people at particular times and places. Do you agree? Discuss.

4. What are the implications of all this for a church deliberately trying to be incarnational? What does all this say about our mission? What does it say about our methods and means?

Study #2
FORM AND FUNCTION

Readings:
ACTF pages 33-91
1 Chr 16:28-30; Lev. 11:45; Rom 12:4-13; Eph 4:11-16; Mt 20:25-28; Mt 28:18-20; Mt 5:14-16.

Overview

"By 'form' I mean those methods, behaviors, and rituals through which the people of God give expression to their life under God—the means they use to carry out the spiritual business to which God has called them. By 'function' I intend to denote the spiritual business itself—those ends which are definitional, fundamental, and central to our identity as God's people" (p. 39).

Discussion Question/Statements/Application

1. Read the story of Mary and Martha (Luke 10:38-42). Both wanted to honor Jesus. Both wanted to 'function' as faithful disciples. But each used a different 'form.' Martha saw to all the preparations. Mary sat at Jesus' feet. Do you see the distinction? Do you understand Jesus' reaction?

2. Review the seven functions of the church (according to chapters 5 and 6). Do you think this list adequately summarizes the church's "essential business"? Should there be other functions added to the list? How do you see these functions in the life of

Christ? In the priorities of first-century Christians?

3. Starting again with the list of seven functions identified in the book, list 'forms' used by Jesus and the early church to enact those functions (e.g., Worship: prayer, song, testimonial, confession, Supper, tongues, etc.).

Study #3
'REACH-UP' FUNCTIONS

Readings:
ACTF pages 55-57, 69-74, Mission Statement on p. 195.
Rev 15:4; 1Pe 1:14-15

Overview

The two primary 'reach-up' functions are worship and holy living. These functions permit us to participate with God. Through worship, we experience God's character and presence. Through holiness, we live out his life.

Discussion Question/Statements/Application

1. What was worship to Jesus and the first Christians? Why did they engage in worship? Don't ask the "how" question yet. Just reflect on the "what" and the "why."

2. Discuss the concept of "worship" versus "going to church." Are these (necessarily) the same thing? When can church get in the way of worship?

3. Which of the following would you identify as important components of true worship? An experience of God ... praise ... humility and confession ... awe ... encouragement ... joy ... power ... communion with the Spirit ... grace and forgiveness.

4. What was holiness to Jesus and the first Christians? Why did they pursue it?

5. Define "holiness." Make sure there is room in your definition for words like "purity," "separateness," "character," and "godliness."

6. We sing, "only Thou art holy," yet we claim that a call to holy living is a basic function of the church. Is holiness an attainable goal for us or are we singing words that we really don't believe?

Study #4
'REACH-UP' FORMS

Readings:
ACTF pages 93-105
Acts 4:23-31; 1Cor 14:20-25; Ro 6:19; 2Cor 7:1; Eph 4:24; Heb 12:14

Overview

If worship and holy living are essential functions of our "reach-up" mission, how do we enact those functions in the 21st century church? What behaviors should we adopt as we live out such core beliefs and commitments?

Discussion Question/Statements/Application

1. Are we free to find fresh forms to enhance ancient functions? Read "Conclusion," pp. 86-87. Do you agree? If not, why not?

2. What spiritual discipline could you embrace to enhance your worship of God? Prayer ... fasting ... Scripture reading ... meditation ... solitude ... journaling ... confession? Notice that each "form" is simply a tool, a means to a greater end. The disciplines (whether personal or public) are never the point. They lead us to something beyond themselves.

3. Brainstorm. If we do have certain freedoms with the forms we use to accomplish godly purposes, what forms could we adopt in order to encourage: an experience of God ... praise ... humility

and confession ... awe ... joy ... power ... communion with the Spirit ... grace and forgiveness?

4. We are called to holiness. What does that look like today? Circumcision? Hand washing? Wearing a veil? Holiness 'forms' must look different in our day and time because holiness always stands in contrast to particular cultures. Make a list of things that set us apart from the world around—attitudes, disciplines, behaviors, perspectives, etc.

Study #5
'REACH-IN' FUNCTIONS

Readings:
ACTF pages 57-60, 74-79, Mission Statement on p. 195.
Gal 6:10; Jn 13:34-35; Rom 12:10; 1Cor 13:1-4; Judges 2:10-19

Overview
"Reaching in" involves building an intimate community of believers and setting up processes for growing mature followers of Christ. These functions permit us to participate with each other in redemptive and effective ways.

Discussion Question/Statements/Application
1. What did fellowship/community mean to Jesus and the early Christians? Why did they put such emphasis on it?

2. Which of the following would you identify as important for building "authentic community"? Humility ... kindness ... intimacy ... forgiveness ... honoring each other ... confession/honesty ... deference ... accountability ... putting others first ... mutual service ... valuing unity. Others?

3. The development of authentic community is a theme that plays powerfully in a post-modern society. Can we do this when

we spend (at most) 4 hours a week with each other? Are we missing an experience of authentic community as a result?

4. "Real disciples are best developed not by educational programs or the reading of books or mission trips but by mentoring relationships with people who take Jesus seriously." Agree?

5. How does your church go about maturing people in Christ?

Study #6
'REACH-IN' FORMS

Readings:
ACTF pages 106-124
Acts 2:42-47; 4:32-35; Eph 4:11-16

Overview

People seem to be hungry for authentic relationships. The PTA, YMCA, Little League, and even Starbucks are channels for community in today's society. As the church builds community and works to mature disciples, are we consciously building something more profound, more radical than Starbucks? If not, can we really claim to be the community God intends us to be?

Discussion Question/Statements/Application

1. We probably feel freer to discover fresh forms for "in-reach" functions than for worship. Would you agree?

2. What are the forms you currently use in your church for creating fellowship and training disciples? Are they working? Are they intentional? Could they be improved?

3. If you were being creative, what forms would you recommend for developing an intimate, warm, intense fellowship of believers? What forms would you suggest for encouraging discipleship in the next generation?

4. Can we have loving community and mentoring relationships without expectations or accountability? Certainly, these can be abused. But can they be avoided? How can we set the bar and help people reach it without undue pressure?

5. Most of us can think of a person that has been a major influence in our lives. Who was that person for you?

Study #7
'REACH-OUT' FUNCTIONS

Readings:
ACTF pages 60-5, 79-86, Mission Statement on p. 195.
Mt 20:25-28; Mt 28:18-20; Mt 5:14-16; Jn 3:16-21.

Overview

As the people of God, we are called to live "in the world," but not be a part of the world. Jesus lived out that principle through service to others, by proclaiming the truth to others and by being salt and light within his circle of influence. The church, as the incarnate body of Christ, is also called to interact with the world in those ways.

Discussion Question/Statements/Application

1. Why did Jesus and the first Christians serve the people around them? Why did they talk about "the hope" they'd found? Why did they try to influence the world in which they lived? What were they attempting to accomplish? Why were these things important to them?

2. Service. Witness. Influence. Which is your church strongest in? Which weakest? Does your congregation have a sense of calling to these functions?

3. In some form or other, all churches serve people. What criteria should a church use in determining who, what, where, when

and how to serve? Are "acts of compassion" justifiable, even if they don't lead to baptisms or world-shaking changes?

4. We've all prayed that "others may see Christ living in us." But do we really expect a significant number of people to come to the cross only because of what they see? Aren't words necessary at some point? What has happened to our witness and our willingness to speak up for Jesus?

5. "Influence" is probably the hardest function to quantify. Name a couple of ways your church could be "salt and light."

Study #8
'REACH-OUT' FORMS

Readings:
ACTF pages 126-139
Prov 25:21-22; Mt 9:35; Ac 5:42; 1Cor 6:9-11

Overview

The church has a responsibility to touch the world, and do it in a provocative, world-changing way. We touch the world through service, witness, and Christian influence. But how? Bus ministries? Soup kitchens? Abortion protests? Boycotts? Clothes closets? Arbor meetings? Techniques effective once upon a time may not be equally effective today. Are we committed enough to these functions to doggedly search for forms that work?

Discussion Question/Statements/Application

1. Summer campaigns, local door-knocking, week-long revival meetings, bus ministries ... all have had an honored place in our history, but few of us are still using these evangelistic forms. Why? List some evangelistic forms that might be more effective. Would your church support these?

2. Is Christian influence a simple by-product of Christian living

or must we deliberately, intentionally set up a contrast with the world by living contrary/counter to the world's norms?

3. Think about the following matters and brainstorm creative ways the church could have an influence on the world's attitudes about race relations ... socioeconomic distinctions ... treatment of enemies ... sexual mores ... materialism ... family.

4. How many non-Christian friends and associates do you have? For the next few days, keep a log of your phone calls and meetings. How many of those people profess faith? How do you know that? If you don't know, do you feel uncomfortable asking them? Do they know of your commitment to Christ?

Study #9
DEVELOPING YOUR OWN MISSION STATEMENT

Readings:
ACTF pages 176-201, (esp. the Mission Statement on p. 195)
Some biblical 'mission statements': Acts 1:8; 1Cor 2:1-4; Mark 1:38; Jn 6:38; 12:46

Overview
Does your church have a mission statement? If so, get it out and read it. Does it inspire you? Does it challenge you? Is there something unique about it or would it be just as fitting if applied to another church down the street?

Discussion Question/Statements/Application
1. Have each person in your discussion group write down what they believe the mission of your congregation IS (as reflected not so much by your current mission statement as by the manner in which the church operates). Now each of you write down what you believe that mission SHOULD BE.

2. It might be instructive to do this same exercise with: a

young adult class ... a college class ... a high school class. Compare the answers. Are there any differences?

3. A good mission statement gives direction ("This is what we're about"), diagnoses problems ("We don't do a very good job in this area"), and helps us stay balanced ("We need to emphasize these kinds of things more"). A good mission statement also lets you say "No." Discuss these characteristics.

4. Play with the seven functions identified in *A Church that Flies*. What kind of mission statement would you write using those seven ideas? What would you add? What would you omit?

5. Developing a mission statement is good. Integrating that statement into the life of a church and implementing it in the church's ministries and structure, is better. Discuss this.

Study #10
THE IMPORTANCE OF BALANCE

Readings:
1Cor 12:1-31; Ro 12:1-8

Overview

Most churches (like most Christians) come to certain functions naturally. They find worship easy ... or outreach ... or community. More to the point, though, most churches come to certain functions hard. Outreach is a challenge. Invigorating worship is a stretch. Which raises the point of "balance."

Discussion Question/Statements/Application

1. "A healthy church is one that pursues balance in its calling to reach up, reach in, and reach out." Discuss this statement. Can a church be healthy if it lacks balance?

2. As you evaluate the various programs or ministries in your

11

congregation, do you find a good balance between reaching up, reaching in, and reaching out? Which functions come easily to your church? Which functions come hard? Why?

3. Most of us acknowledge the importance of the "body" metaphor in talking about the church—one body, many members working together, one head (Jesus). And we recognize that, though different parts have different functions, all are equally important. What does this metaphor say to us about "balance" and a "diversity" of ministries?

4. Effectiveness is maximized through balance. Should all seven functions of the church be given the same weight? What happens when certain functions get more focus while others get less? What does this do to the "body"?

5. Can a church incarnate Christ and lack balance? Did he?

Study #11
CHANGE & THE CHURCH

Readings:
ACTF pages 141-174

Overview

The more things change, the more they remain the same.
Old French Proverb

The significant problems we face cannot be solved at the same level of thinking we were at when we created them.
Albert Einstein

If you continue doing the same thing, you will continue getting the same results. Business axiom

Everything is subject to change. In fact, in these hectic times, everything seems eager to change. Many of us are suffering from what Alvin Toffler calls "Future Shock." We are reeling from the

12

effects, the pace, and the invasiveness of change. In fact, some of the angst about change in churches may be fueled by our sense that, if every other part of our lives is out of control, at least we can hang on to something stable and unchanging in church.

Discussion Question/Statements/Application

1. Are you suffering from "Future Shock"? Is your church?

2. In business, if you aren't continually changing, then you are falling behind. To stay with the status quo when all other factors are changing condemns you to diminishing returns. Does this same principle apply to church?

3. How do the quotes above apply to the church?

4. As times change and as culture changes, what is required of the church to "keep up"? What changes are demanded? What changes should be resisted? How can you know which is which?

IF YOU'VE GOT QUESTIONS

Here at Otter Creek, we've been working hard to apply the principles of this book. We've had successes and failures, problems and victories. You may want to talk more about certain issues. You may need to ask questions. So feel free to contact us. We'd be honored to open our church life to you and put you in touch with ministers, administrative staff, elders, ministry coordinators (deacons), and various members of the congregation.

You might even be interested in having one or more of this group come to talk with your leadership group. If so, we'd be eager to partner with you in this way.

We certainly make no claim of having all the right answers. We have our own problems and frustrations. We continue to learn and grow. But our prayer is that we keep our eyes on Jesus and that every decision we make and change we implement is in keeping with his will for our lives.

The Otter Creek Family of Faith
5253 Granny White Pike
Nashville, TN 37220
(615) 373-1782
office@ottercreek.org
www.ottercreek.org